Steps to Follow

1 Brainstorm and list different shapes. Ask children to name animals. Discuss the shapes that might be used to create them. A horse, for example, might be made from an oval body and head, rectangular neck and legs, and triangular hooves and ears. Draw some examples on the chalkboard.

2 Have each child choose an animal and experiment with several designs on a sheet of scrap paper. Encourage children to use many different shapes.

3 Draw the outline of the animal with black crayon on the art paper.

4 Paint the animal with the primed watercolors. Children may use many different colors. Instruct them to rinse the brush in water after each color change.

5 Set the painting aside to dry.

step 3

How to prime a watercolor set

Before using the watercolors, put a few drops of water on each color to soften the paints. The water will loosen the pigment and give richer color.

step 4

ArtWorks for Kids • EMC 761

Action Painting

Create an abstract painting using unconventional methods of application.

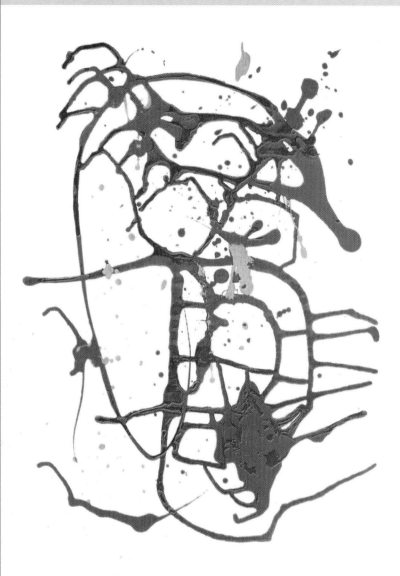

Let's Talk About It

What kinds of things can you paint with?

Why is this method called action painting?

What is the best part of action painting?

Discuss how feelings can be expressed through color. Blue and purple may give a sad feeling, while yellow and pink denote happiness. Red and black can show anger.

Vocabulary

abstract

action painting

contrast

Materials

- large paper at least 18" x 24" (46 x 61 cm) per child
- thinned tempera paint in squeeze bottles, spray bottles, cups
- brushes

Project Notes

- This project may be done by individual children or as a group project, using a large wall-size sheet of paper or material such as a bed sheet.

- Prepare a work area before beginning. Do this project outdoors if possible, where paint can be easily cleaned up. Smocks are advisable, as this can be a messy project.

- Show prints of famous action painters such as Jackson Pollock. Check your school or public library for prints or art books.

Contents

About ArtWorks for Kids

Art **does** work for kids!

- Art nurtures creativity and abstract thought
- Art gives children a unique way to express themselves
- Art helps children relate to culture
- Art is fun

The projects in this book were developed to introduce children to a variety of art media and techniques. We recommend that you do each project yourself ahead of time to better anticipate any special assistance that may be needed.

Follow-up will enrich the art experience. After a project is completed, discuss the artwork. Allow children to critique their own works by finding something they like and something they don't like about the finished product.

Each of the 68 projects follow the same two-page layout.

art terms related to that particular project

a materials list

illustrated step-by-step instructions

a full-color illustration of a completed project

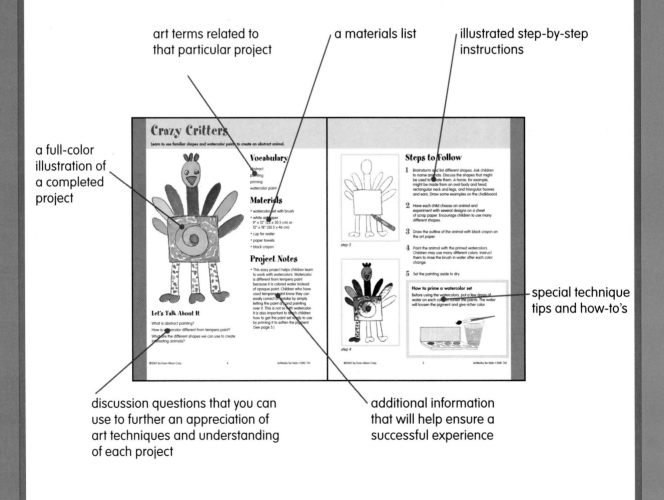

special technique tips and how-to's

discussion questions that you can use to further an appreciation of art techniques and understanding of each project

additional information that will help ensure a successful experience

Painting

Crazy Critters

Learn to use familiar shapes and watercolor paints to create an abstract animal.

Let's Talk About It

What is abstract painting?

How is watercolor different from tempera paint?

What are the different shapes we can use to create interesting animals?

Vocabulary

abstract

painting

priming

watercolor paint

Materials

- watercolor set with brush
- white art paper 9" x 12" (23 x 30.5 cm) or 12" x 18" (30.5 x 46 cm)
- cup for water
- paper towels
- black crayon

Project Notes

- This easy project helps children learn to work with watercolors. Watercolor is different from tempera paint because it is colored water instead of opaque paint. Children who have used tempera paint know they can easily correct a mistake by simply letting the paint dry and painting over it. This is not so with watercolor. It is also important to teach children how to get the paint set ready to use by priming it to soften the pigment. (See page 5.)

Steps to Follow

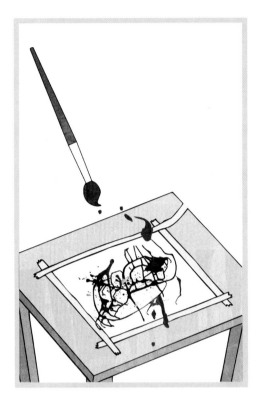

1 Prepare the paints ahead of time. Don't thin the paint too much, just enough to pass through the squeeze or spray bottles. Make a sufficient amount so you won't have to stop once the artists are in action.

2 Tape the paper to a horizontal surface.

3 Let children have fun spraying, splattering, or squirting the paint.

4 Time each artist or group of artists and let them paint for approximately 3 to 5 minutes. It is important to work fast to keep the paper from becoming saturated.

Which Colors?

What kind of color palette will you offer children? The choice of colors in this painting is important.

Provide children with access to a color wheel. Discuss primary and secondary colors. Which ones will be the most effective in this medium of painting? Introduce the concept of contrast here as a way of creating drama in a painting.

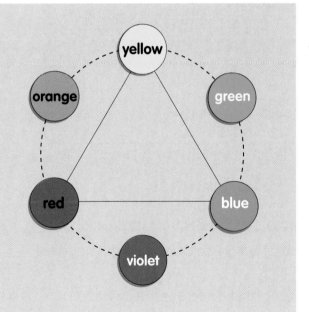

Color Blocks

Create a painting using geometric shapes and complementary colors.

Vocabulary

complementary colors

Cubism

geometric design

Materials

- white paper
  12" x 18" (30.5 x 46 cm)
- tempera paint
  (various colors in cups)
- brushes
- black marker (broad tip)
- pencil
- ruler or straight edge

Project Notes

- This technique was originally developed by several artists in Paris in the early 1900s. They were called Cubists because of their frequent use of geometric motifs. Talk about Cubism and show examples of paintings by Piet Mondrian. Discuss how Mondrian liked to paint with straight lines and right angles.

- Discuss complementary colors and why they are effective in this sort of painting.

- Set up groups of children to work with each other and share supplies.

Let's Talk About It

How does Cubism differ from abstractionism?

Do complementary colors work with or against each other?

Does your painting seem restful or busy?

How does using black marker clarify the artwork?

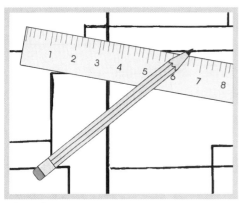

step 2

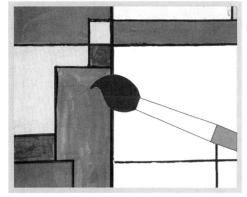

step 3

Steps to Follow

1 Decide whether to work on the horizontal or vertical orientation of the paper (landscape or portrait).

2 Develop the design by sketching with a pencil, using a ruler or straight edge. Try not to divide the design directly in half on the paper. Add interest by grouping smaller shapes in one area and larger ones around them.

3 Paint each section of the design using complementary colors. Encourage children to leave some white space to keep the painting bright and airy.

4 When the painting is completely dry, children may use a black marker and ruler to redraw the original pencil lines.

Complementary Colors

Complementary colors are pairs of colors that are opposite each other on the color wheel. Children need to experiment with these colors to understand that they are powerful when used together. Complementary colors may appear to vibrate when placed side by side in a painting.

red - green

blue - orange

yellow - violet

Note: Pages 27 and 28 contain an explanation of the color wheel and a reproducible color wheel.

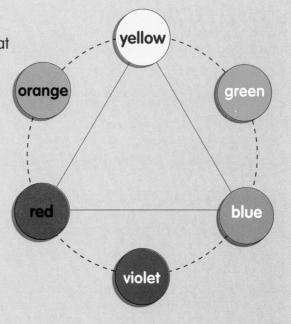

ArtWorks for Kids • EMC 761

Stained-Glass Window

Create a painting that looks like a stained-glass window by using fingerpaint and tissue paper.

Let's Talk About It

What medium was used in this painting?

Why use fingers instead of brushes in this project?

What gives this painting a transparent look?

Vocabulary

medium

technique

transparent

Materials

- white tissue paper (any size)
- tempera paints
- liquid starch
- black marker
- construction paper (for frame)
- bowls

Project Notes

- This simple project offers experience with finger painting on a more sophisticated level.

- Show some samples of stained-glass windows. Point out the colored glass and the lead that separates each color and helps hold the glass together. Discuss the wonder of the transparent effect when the glass is held up to the light.

- Set up a work area and have children wear smocks. Choose an area for drying paintings before you start. Work with one small group at a time.

Steps to Follow

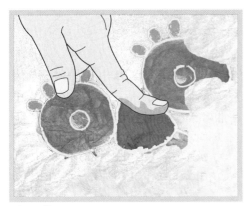

step 2

1 Lay the tissue paper flat on the table. Decide what to paint.

2 Using fingers and the paints, create a picture using lots of different colors.

3 Set the painting aside to dry. When the painting is completely dry, trace around every shape with a black marker to resemble the lead in a real stained-glass window.

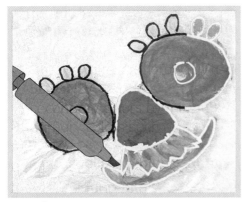

step 3

4 Create a frame for the painting with construction paper. Hang these paintings in a window and enjoy the transparent effect.

How to mix the finger paint

Use 1/2 cup (120 ml) of tempera to 1/4 cup (60 ml) of starch. Mix a bowl of color for every color on the color wheel.

How to frame a transparent picture

Cut two pieces of construction paper 4" (10 cm) wider and longer than the painted image. Cut out the center of one piece, leaving a 2" (5 cm) border around the outside. Paste the tissue paper painting between the paper pieces to create a frame effect.

step 4

Vegetable Bouquet

Watercolor techniques combine with tempera vegetable prints to create a vibrant still life.

Let's Talk About It

What is a still life?

How can painting and printing be used in the same piece of artwork?

How is watercolor different from tempera paint?

Vocabulary

background	gradated wash	printing
foreground	painting	technique

Materials

- watercolor set with brush
- cup for water
- white art paper
- salt
- celery stalk (cut close to bottom)
- bell pepper (sliced crosswise to form flower shape)
- onion (sliced crosswise to show texture)
- flat dishes for tempera
- tempera paint (for flower prints)

Project Notes

- This project uses the watercolor techniques of gradated wash, wet on wet, wet on dry, and using salt to add texture. Printing with tempera paint is combined with the watercolor techniques. Practice the watercolor and printing techniques before starting the project.

- Set up all of the materials before starting. To prevent accidents, children should remain seated while painting.

- Try not to use excessive amounts of water. Paintings can become very soggy with too much moisture.

Steps to Follow

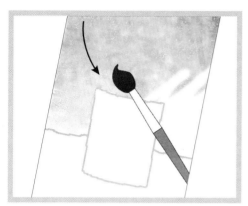
step 2

step 4

step 6

1 Children should turn their papers to the vertical position. After priming their watercolor sets, have them draw in a simple shape for a vase and a table line behind the vase.

2 Brush clean water from the top of the paper to the table line, leaving the vase area dry. Drop a few brush loads of different colors onto the water (wet on wet technique). Colors will be fuzzy and create a background for the flowers.

3 While the paint is wet, sprinkle salt in different areas to add texture. Let the painting dry thoroughly before removing the excess salt.

4 Brush clean water on the vase area. Lay in paint starting on the left side. Using vertical strokes, continue to paint water on the rest of the vase to create a gradated wash. The vase should be dark on the left side and light on the right side.

5 Paint the table area with another color (wet on dry technique). Let the paint dry.

6 Pour several bright colors of tempera paint into flat plates or trays. Dip the end of the celery into the paint and print several "flowers." Continue the same process with the other vegetables to create a "bouquet."

7 Using watercolor, add green stems and leaves.

ArtWorks for Kids • EMC 761

Fish Pond

Develop a water scene by combining watercolor with printing.

Vocabulary

impression

pigment

technique

Materials

- watercolor paper
  9" x 12" (23 x 30.5 cm) or
  12" x 18" (30.5 x 46 cm)
- watercolor set
- brushes (large and small)
- plastic wrap (enough to cover paper generously)
- tempera paint (black)
- small fresh fish
- newspapers or paper towels
- sponge for cleanup
- bucket of water

Let's Talk About It

What technique gave the impression of moving water?

What do the fish prints add to this painting?

Does the placement of the fish suggest movement?

Project Notes

- Set up a station for printing and let a few children print at a time.
- Wash the fish in a bucket of water and then dry them between each print so that the texture of the fins and scales will show.

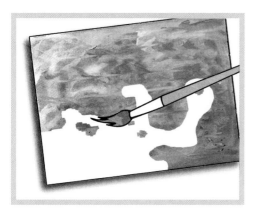

step 2

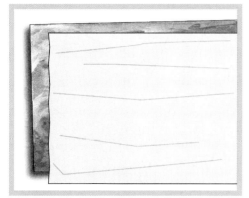

step 3

step 6

Steps to Follow

1 Wet watercolor paper generously with water.

2 Prime the watercolor set. Then drop large brush loads of blue and green pigment onto the paper until it is covered.

3 Lay plastic wrap over the wet, painted paper. Let wrinkles and bumps remain. DO NOT smooth plastic. Tap the plastic wrap down gently and let the paint dry completely.

4 Remove the plastic wrap.

5 Dry the fish with paper towels and paint one side with black tempera.

6 Print the fish by placing the paint side of the fish onto the painted paper and pressing with newspaper or paper towels. Add as many fish prints as needed to complete the design.

Sand Painting

Native American sand paintings provide a lesson in design symmetry.

Vocabulary

asymmetrical   pictograph

design   symmetry

medium   texture

Materials

- cornmeal
- food coloring
- construction paper 6" x 9" (15 x 23 cm)
- pencil
- glue
- bowls (for cornmeal and glue)
- spoon
- brush or cotton swab
- smocks

Let's Talk About It

What kinds of media can be used in painting?

Why is it important to plan a design before beginning to paint?

What is the difference between symmetrical and asymmetrical designs?

How are sand paintings different from other traditional ways of painting?

How does the texture of the sand painting add feeling to the finished piece?

Project Notes

- If possible, show photographs of Native American artwork. Discuss how Native Americans use pictographs to represent ideas in their art. Pictographs tell a story.

- Give children the opportunity to experiment with symmetrical designs before beginning an actual project.

- Have children wear smocks when working with food coloring.

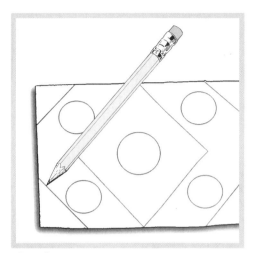

step 1

step 2

step 3

Steps to Follow

1 Fold the paper in half to find the center. Open the paper and lay it flat. Draw a symmetrical design (keep it simple). *Symmetrical* means that the design will be balanced on both sides of the fold.

2 Using a brush or cotton swab, paint one area at a time with glue.

3 Starting with the darker colors, sprinkle the "sand" mixture liberally onto each design area.

4 Let each color set a few seconds, and then lift the paper and gently shake any excess sand back into the bowl. Continue filling in the design (ending with the lightest color) until the area is entirely covered.

5 Let the painting dry completely.

Our sand painting will be done with dyed cornmeal.

Mix cornmeal and food coloring ahead of time or let children make the "sand" for this project. Pour 1/2 cup (100 g) of cornmeal into a bowl for each color. Add a few drops of food coloring and mix thoroughly with a spoon. Do not saturate cornmeal, but make the colors vivid.

Dancing Monkeys

This project imitates the art of Wang Yani and the Oriental style of painting using a limited palette.

Vocabulary

limited palette   xieyi

Materials

- watercolor set
- brushes (thick and thin)
- 2 pieces of paper per child 6" x 18" (15 x 46 cm)
- cups for water
- paper towels

Project Notes

- Prime only the red and black watercolors. Make the watercolor very "soupy."
- Children need to practice with large and small brushes. Thick brushstrokes are best for the monkeys' arms and legs, and thin strokes for fingers, toes, and details.

Let's Talk About It

Why are Chinese-style paintings so different from European artwork?

Do all paintings tell a story?

What mood do the Chinese paintings convey?

Share the Art of Wang Yani

Introduce the artist Wang Yani by showing prints of her work. Point out that she uses only simple brushstrokes and creates movement in her pictures by the way she paints the elbows and knees of her subjects.

 ArtWorks for Kids • EMC 761

Steps to Follow

step 2

step 3

step 4

1 Demonstrate for children how to use simple brushstrokes to create monkey body parts such as those shown on page 18. Use both thick and thin brushes. You might gather children around you or paint on the overhead projector.

2 Children use one sheet of paper to practice strokes. Encourage children to try many different techniques for creating separate monkey body parts. They are using only black paint at this point.

3 When children are comfortable with using the brushes, start the final painting with black on another sheet of paper. Place the paper either vertically or horizontally. The monkeys may dance and move across the paper.

4 After the black paint is dry, use red paint to add the mouth, eyes, nose, and other details.

ArtWorks for Kids • EMC 761

Impasto Painting

Investigate texture in a painting by creating a still life using the medium of impasto.

Let's Talk About It

What is a still life?

How is impasto different from watercolor?

How does the thickness of the medium add to the feeling of the finished project?

Does the subject seem more real or solid than it would if painted with watercolors? Why?

Does the texture created from the impasto make the subject more interesting? How?

Vocabulary

impasto

medium

still life

texture

Materials

- tempera paint (various colors)
- paste or dry soap flakes (you may grate bar soap)
- fruit or flowers
- cups
- spoon
- brushes (one for each color)
- cardboard 9" x 12" (23 x 30.5 cm)
- pencil

Project Notes

- Show prints of Vincent Van Gogh's work. Discuss how he used color and texture to create these rich works of art.

- Explain that in the impasto technique, a paste-like substance is added to the paint to extend it while not changing the intensity of the color. This is cost effective, as paints are expensive. Also, the thickness of the impasto adds texture to the painting and gives it more of a 3-D effect.

- Vincent Van Gogh's *Sunflowers* is an example of this type of painting.

Steps to Follow

1 After discussing the impasto technique, set up a display of fruit or flowers for children to sketch on a piece of cardboard. Keep it simple.

step 1

2 Have children paint the drawn picture with the impasto. Encourage them to leave the lumps as they paint. Continue to paint until every part of the painting has been completed.

3 After the paint has dried, have children outline the different parts of the painting with black tempera paint for more definition. The goal in this project is to gain experience in a very old medium and see how texture can add depth to a painting.

step 2

To mix impasto

Mix the impasto paint before starting. Let the children be involved in the process. Have small groups of children share the paints.

Mix tempera and paste or dry soap flakes in this ratio: 1/2 cup (120 ml) tempera to 1/3 cup (80 g) paste or soap flakes. Leave the lumps to add texture to the painting. Make several cups of each color.

step 3

Snowy Forest

Watercolor techniques create a landscape of shadowy birch trees.

Vocabulary

background   masking

foreground   sponging

landscape   wet on wet technique

Materials

- watercolor set with brush
- watercolor paper
  9" x 12" (23 x 30.5 cm)
- cup for water
- paper towels
- 7" (18 cm) masking tape strips
  (5 per child)
- toothbrush
- white tempera (in cups)
- small sponge pieces

Let's Talk About It

What is a landscape?

How is painting different from printing?

What is the proper way to use a watercolor set and brush?

How can shadows add dimension to a painting?

Project Notes

- Have children prime their watercolor sets to soften the pigment.
- Model the masking and sponging techniques they will be using.
- Talk about foreground and background in a painting.
- Don't let the children overwork their paintings. Help them to know when to stop by taking periodic breaks to reflect on what has been done so far.
- Look at photos of birch trees so children can become familiar with the pale trunks.

Steps to Follow

steps 1 & 2

steps 3, 4, & 5

steps 6 & 7

1 Take the strips of masking tape and tear them lengthwise. Place the torn strips on the watercolor paper to create the outlines of trees in a forest. Make sure the edges are pressed down.

2 Using water, sweep the brush across the paper and the tape. Wash blue and purple paint on the background. Allow the colors to mix freely. The foreground is left white to resemble the snowy ground.

3 While the paper is still wet, lightly drop in shadows with brown paint at the base of the tree trunks. The shadows should all be on the same side of trees.

4 When the painting is completely dry, gently remove the tape. The white spaces left will be the birch tree trunks.

5 Add details to the birch trees with brown paint and the point of a brush. Make a dot-dash pattern applied at random. Avoid making the trees look striped. Children may add weeds and grasses in the snow at the same time.

6 Now use a piece of sponge dipped in dark green watercolor to make evergreen bushes around the base of the trees. Don't overdo it.

7 A snowflake effect can be created by using a toothbrush that has been dipped in white tempera paint. Flick "snow" over the painting by quickly pulling the thumb over the bristles and splattering the paint on the paper.

Abstract Watercolor

Create an abstract painting by experimenting with several watercolor techniques.

Vocabulary

abstract

design

primary colors

secondary colors

technique

Materials

- scrap paper for practice
- watercolor paper
  9" x 12" (23 x 30.5 cm)
- watercolor set with brush
- sponge
- a straw
- cup for water
- tissue & paper towel
- plastic wrap
- wax candle
- salt

Let's Talk About It

How are abstract paintings different from realistic paintings?

Abstract paintings may be a painting of an emotion or a sound. What emotion does your painting reflect?

How are watercolor techniques used to create impressions of objects such as stars or feathers?

Project Notes

- Let children work at their own pace. Let them "play" with all the techniques before they make their final picture. Encourage them to title their work. Children who feel unsure about creating art are often freed by abstract painting.

ArtWorks for Kids • EMC 761

Steps to Follow

wet on wet   *wet on dry*

salt   *blowing*

plastic wrap

sponge

gradated wash

1 Model these watercolor techniques for the children:

- Salt sprinkled on wet paint will give a starry effect when dry.

- Cover wet paint with plastic wrap and let it dry, then remove plastic to get a watery look.

- Dip a sponge in pigment and print on paper to create a lacy effect.

- Draw with a wax candle, then brush paint over the top for a "resist" or masking technique.

- Blow across wet paint with a straw to get a spidery look.

- Wet the paper with clear water and then drop pigment into the pools for a feathery look called "blooms."

2 Have children prime their paint sets by putting a drop of water on each color to soften the pigment.

3 Allow children enough time to try various techniques until they become relaxed and comfortable with them.

4 Have children create an abstract painting using one or more of the techniques they have learned.

     ArtWorks for Kids • EMC 761

Mini-Abstracts

Children choose sections of their abstract watercolor to create mini-abstracts for display.

Materials

- abstract watercolor, (see pages 24 and 25)
- small white file cards (3 per child)
- viewfinder
- glue
- scissors
- pencil

How to make a viewfinder

Cut out a window approximately 1 1/2" x 3" (4 x 7.5 cm) in the center of a standard white file card. Make several of these viewfinders for children to share.

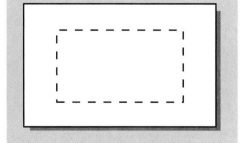

Steps to Follow

1 Children use a viewfinder to zero in on interesting sections of the abstract watercolors created in the previous lesson. Caution them to choose three sections before marking and cutting.

2 Trace around the rectangular opening of the viewfinder with pencil to mark each of the three sections chosen. Cut out each section.

3 Glue each mini-abstract to the center of a white file card.

4 Create a display area where children can share their miniatures.

 ArtWorks for Kids • EMC 761

The Color Wheel

Reproduce the color wheel on page 28 for children. Have them color the wheel as you explain the meanings of the terms below.

Primary Colors

Red, yellow, and blue are called **PRIMARY** colors. Primary colors cannot be made by mixing colors together. You can use the primary colors to make other colors.

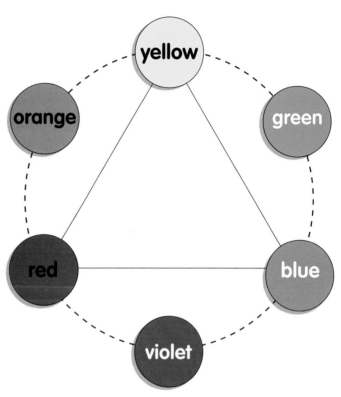

Secondary Colors

Green, violet, and orange are called **SECONDARY** colors. You can create the secondary colors by mixing two adjacent primary colors such as:

yellow + blue = green

blue + red = violet

red + yellow = orange

Complementary Colors

Colors that are opposite one another on the color wheel are called **COMPLEMENTARY** colors. These color combinations are especially powerful when used together.

red - green

yellow - violet

blue - orange

Intermediate Colors

INTERMEDIATE colors are yellow green, blue green, blue violet, red violet, red orange, and yellow orange. These colors are created by mixing each color together such as:

yellow + green = yellow green

red + orange = red orange

blue + violet = blue violet

Color Wheel

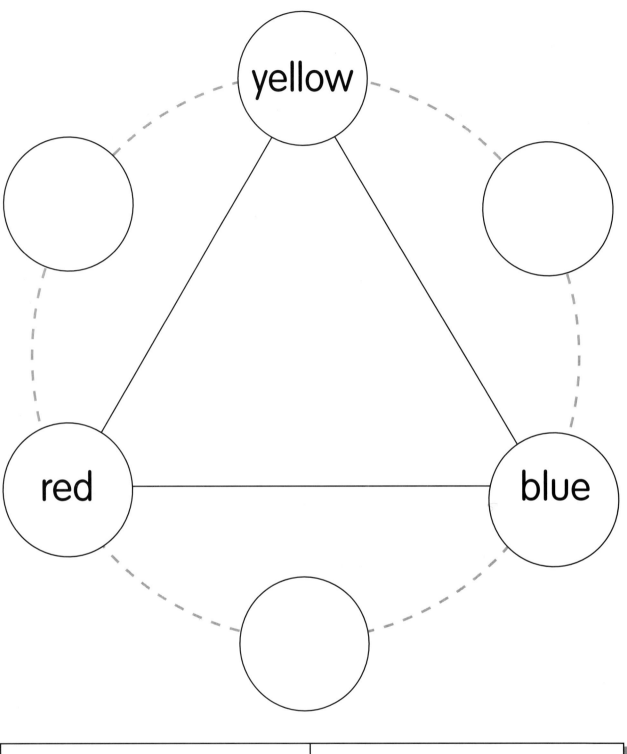

Primary Colors	**Secondary Colors**
• red • blue • yellow	• orange • violet • green

Weaving

ArtWorks for Kids • EMC 761

Paper Mats

This basic project shows children how to weave a paper mat using complementary colors.

Vocabulary

complementary colors   weaving

warp   weft

Materials

- construction paper in red, green, yellow, purple, blue, orange—
  9" x 12" (23 x 30.5 cm), 1 per child
- 1" x 9" (2.5 x 23 cm), 11 strips per child
- scissors
- glue or paste
- ruler
- pencil

Project Notes

- Use these mats to decorate the room or as place mats for a class party.
- Explain a loom to the children. A loom is a device on which cloth is produced by interweaving thread or yarn at right angles. The threads on the loom go in two different directions: vertically and horizontally. The vertical threads are called warp threads. The horizontal threads are called weft.

Let's Talk About It

How is weaving different from painting?

What does weaving have in common with sculpture?

What materials other than paper could you use to weave this project?

(Explain how Native Americans used grasses to weave mats.)

How did the use of complementary colors help in doing this project?

Steps to Follow

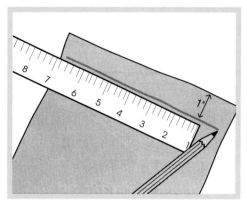

step 2

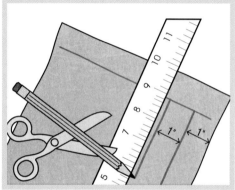

step 3

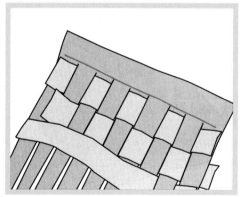

step 4

1 After discussing complementary colors (see below), each child chooses a sheet of construction paper in one color and 11 strips of paper in its complementary color.

2 Lay the sheet of paper vertically on the table. Use a ruler to measure 1" (2.5 cm) from the top and mark with a pencil line. This will be where the cut lines will stop.

3 Measure across the width of the paper. Draw vertical lines every inch (2.5 cm). Cut on these lines. These cut lines will form the warp lines for this weaving.

4 Place the cut sheet of paper on the table and begin weaving with the precut paper strips. Slide each woven strip up next to the previous one.

5 Carefully glue or paste the last strip to the warp ends to keep everything in place.

Complementary colors

Introduce the color wheel (see page 27).
Help children locate the complementary colors.
Complementary colors are opposite each other on the color wheel:

red	-	green
yellow	-	violet
blue	-	orange

Woven Landscape

Irregular woven strips suggest landscape features. Children create an outdoor scene in the center.

Vocabulary

landscape

warp

weaving

weft

Materials

- construction paper sheets
  9" x 12" (23 x 30.5 cm)
- construction paper strips in two
  contrasting colors
  5" x 1" (13 x 2.5 cm)
- scissors
- crayons
- glue or paste
- ruler

Project Notes

- Young children may need help measuring and making the initial cuts in the background paper.
- Offer a variety of colored papers and let children choose one sheet of paper for a background color and contrasting strips of two other colors.

Let's Talk About It

What types of materials can be used in a weaving?

How can a weaving tell a story?

How do the wavy cut lines add movement to the weaving?

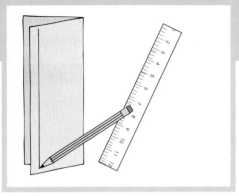

step 1

step 2

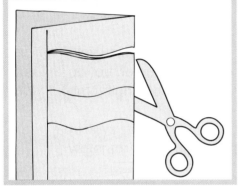

step 4

steps 5 & 6

Steps to Follow

1 Fold the sheet of construction paper in half. Make a pencil line 1" (2.5 cm) from the open edge.

2 Starting at the fold, cut across the paper with curved lines. Stop at the pencil line each time. Cut approximately 4 lines in the top third and 4 lines in the bottom third of the paper. Do not make cuts in the center.

3 Open the paper and lay it flat on the table. Smooth out the crease made when folding.

4 Draw and color a simple outdoor scene with crayon in the center area of the paper—perhaps a tree, or a sailboat with clouds and birds.

5 Begin weaving strips of paper through the slits. Use one color of strips for the top and the other color of strips for the bottom. Do not cover the drawing.

6 Secure the paper strips with a drop of glue on each end when finished.

Tissue Weaving

Create a stained-glass window effect using transparent tissue paper and basic weaving skills.

Let's Talk About It

How are new colors created in this weaving technique?

Can weaving colored yarns side by side appear to be an illusion of different colors?

(The eye seems able to mix color all on its own. Red yarn woven next to a yellow yarn can create orange when viewed from a distance.)

Vocabulary

primary colors	transparent
secondary colors	warp
shuttle	weft

Materials

- construction paper for frames
  9" x 12" (23 x 30.5 cm)

- white paper
  9" x 12" (23 x 30.5 cm)

- scissors and a ruler

- tissue paper strips
  2" x 12" (5 x 30.5 cm)
  1 blue   1 red   1 yellow

- tissue paper cut in strips
  2" x 9" (5 x 23 cm)
  1 blue   2 red   2 yellow

- glue or paste

Project Notes

- Precut the frames for younger children. (See step 5.)

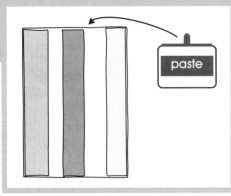

step 2

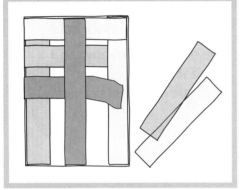

step 3

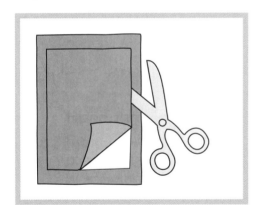

step 5

step 6

Steps to Follow

1 Start by placing the white paper vertically on the table.

2 Glue 1 red, 1 blue, and 1 yellow 12" (30.5 cm) strip side by side starting at the top of the paper to create the warp. Glue down only the tops.

3 Start weaving the shorter colored strips through the warp, starting with yellow and continuing with red, then blue, red again, and finishing with yellow. These are the weft. Glue the ends of each strip to the white paper to keep them in place.

4 When all strips are woven and glued in place, glue the bottom of the warp pieces to the bottom of the paper.

5 Mark a 1" (2.5 cm) border around the outside edge of the colored construction paper. Cut on this line to create a frame for the picture.

6 Place the frame piece over the woven paper and glue in place.

7 Hold the finished project up to the light to see how mixing two primary colors will result in a secondary color wherever the two cross one another. Red and yellow woven together will produce orange. Yellow and blue will produce green. Blue and red will produce purple.

ArtWorks for Kids • EMC 761

Art Portfolios

Make an art portfolio from woven corrugated paper.

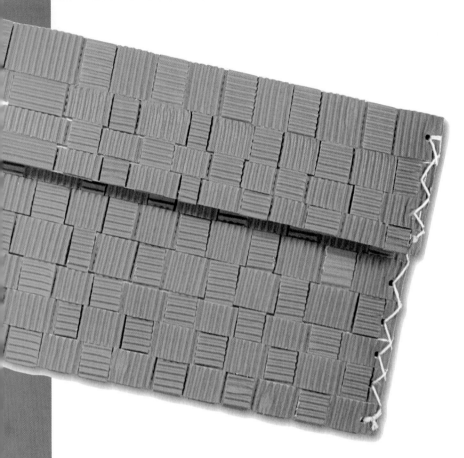

Vocabulary

texture

warp

weft

Materials

- corrugated bulletin board paper strips
  2" x 22" (5 x 56 cm) and
  2" x 28" (5 x 71 cm) strips

- posterboard
  22" x 28" (56 x 71 cm)
  one per project

- stapler

- glue gun with glue (optional)

- hole punch

- heavy yarn

Let's Talk About It

What types of materials can be used to weave?

What is the loom in this project?

How does the texture help in creating a pattern on the portfolio?

How is sewing like weaving?

Project Notes

- A lot of space is needed to work on this project, so try sitting on the floor to work.

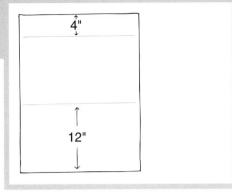

step 1

steps 2 & 3

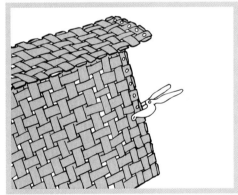

steps 5 & 6

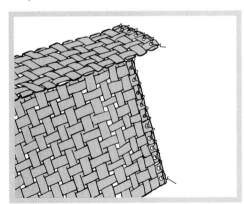

step 7

Steps to Follow

1 Place the posterboard vertically on a flat surface. Measure 4" (10 cm) down from the top and draw a line. This will be the flap. Then draw a line at 12" (30.5 cm) up from the bottom. This will be the fold to create the pocket of the portfolio. Flip the posterboard over, keeping it vertical.

2 Staple the long strips of paper, corrugated side up, side by side to the top and bottom of the posterboard. Let any extra paper hang over the top edge.

3 Begin weaving the shorter weft strips, smooth side up, back and forth through the warp strips. Staple each strip in place after it is pushed close together. A checkerboard pattern of textures should be visible.

4 After the weaving is complete, flip it over and turn down any pieces hanging over the top of the portfolio. Glue or staple these pieces in place.

5 Fold the portfolio on the line drawn 12" (30.5 cm) from the bottom, leaving the flap up.

6 While holding the sides together, punch holes through both layers along both sides. An adult will need to punch the holes for younger children, as it takes some strength to go through both layers of woven paper.

7 Tie a strip of heavy yarn to one side and sew the sides together. Complete both sides. Fold the flap portion down to close the portfolio.

ArtWorks for Kids • EMC 761

Weaving Bookmarks

Make a yarn bookmark using basic weaving skills.

Vocabulary

loom	warp
patterning	weft
shuttle	

Materials

- cardboard loom (see below)
- yarn cut in 2 1/2-yard lengths (2.25 m), two different colors per child
- plastic forks, one per child
- scissors
- yardstick or meterstick

Project Notes

- If possible, show weavings from different cultures or take a trip to a museum to enjoy Native American weavings. Use this project as a supplement to a social studies lesson on different cultures.

Let's Talk About It

How is this cardboard loom different from a loom used in making a rug?

How do the color and texture of the materials make a weaving different from a painting?

What are the similarities between painting and weaving?

Making Cardboard Looms:

Cut cardboard into 5" x 8" (13 x 20 cm) looms. Use a pair of scissors to cut at least six 1/4" (0.6 cm) notches in each end.

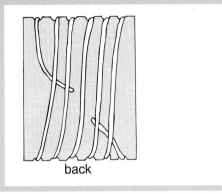

back

step 2

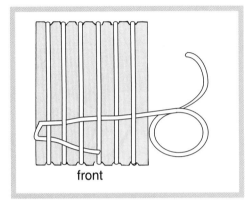

front

step 3

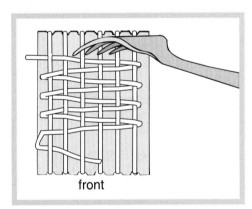

front

step 5

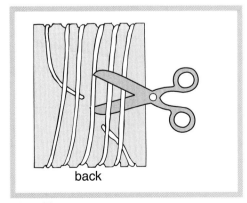

back

step 7

Steps to Follow

1 Tape the yardstick (or meterstick) on the table next to the yarn. Let children choose the colors they wish to use. They are to measure the yarn along the measuring stick and cut the pieces into 2 1/2-yard (2.25 m) lengths. Use one color yarn for the warp and another color for the weft.

2 Attach the yarn to the loom by holding the end with one finger about halfway and wrapping from top to bottom, making sure to slide yarn into each notch. Make the tension firm but not rigid. (When the weaving is finished, you may cut this warp string, leaving a few inches so it will not unravel.)

3 Begin the weaving process by attaching the weft yarn. Start in the middle of the warp and weave the yarn in and out of the warp strings using your finger as the shuttle to carry the yarn.

4 Proceed to weave. Work the yarn back and forth through the warp, alternating rows over and under on each new pass.

5 After each pass, pack down the yarn gently with the fork.

6 When the weaving is complete, weave the last bit of yarn back through the warp, ending in the center. This keeps the yarn from unraveling without crimping the weaving with a knot.

7 To remove the weaving from the loom, turn the loom over and cut the warp strings in the center. Use a bit of extra yarn to tie the strings together with a knot on each end.

     ArtWorks for Kids • EMC 761

Paper Baskets

Weave a basket using a monochromatic color scheme.

Vocabulary

monochromatic

warp

weaving

weft

Materials

- construction paper
  9" x 9" (23 x 23 cm)
- construction paper strips
  1" x 13" (2.5 x 33 cm)
- glue or paste
- ruler
- pencil
- scissors
- stapler

Project Notes

- These baskets are small enough to be very useful and don't take up too much space. Use the baskets in the classroom for crayons, manipulatives, chalk, etc.

Let's Talk About It

How is weaving a basket different from weaving a blanket?

How are they the same?

How are variations created even in a monochromatic color scheme?

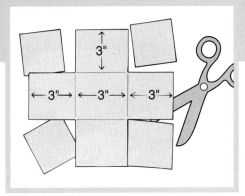

step 1

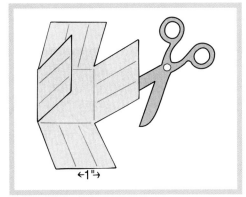

step 2

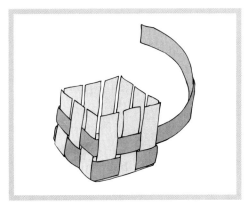

step 4

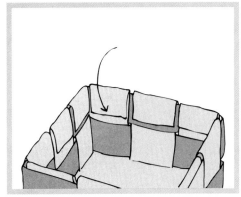

step 5

Steps to Follow

1 Lay the sheet of paper flat on the table. Use a ruler to measure 3" (8 cm) from each edge of the paper. Draw a line at each of these points. Cut out the corner boxes.

2 The four pieces of paper sticking out will create the sides of the basket. Measure each section into 1" (2.5 cm) strips and cut from the outer edge to the center line. There will be three 1" (2.5 cm) strips on each side attached to the center square.

3 Fold these strips up to form the sides of the basket. This is the warp.

4 The 1" x 13" (2.5 x 33 cm) strips will be the weft. Start at a bottom corner and weave in and out between the warp strips. Glue the ends together after each row to keep them in place. Continue weaving until you reach the top of the basket.

5 You may fold the top edges of the warp over to the inside and glue them down. To make a more finished edge, glue an extra strip inside the top edge.

6 If desired, staple on a paper handle.

What is a monochromatic color scheme?

Monochromatic refers to the use of a single color in an art project. That color, however, may be of several different intensities. Children may choose to use light and dark green or two shades of blue. It is important to realize that even a monochromatic color scheme can be interesting and varied.

Broom Art

Learn three-dimensional weaving techniques by making a broom.

Vocabulary

shuttle

square knot

warp

weft

Materials

- broom straw cut in varying lengths from 12" (30.5 cm) to 16" (41 cm)
- strong garden shears or scissors
- twine, yarn, or sisal cut in 30" (76 cm) and 24" (61 cm) lengths

Project Notes

- Brooms may be made from straw, cornhusks, wheat straw, or any type of tall grass.
- Secure the straw clusters with rubber bands or clothespins while weaving. Remove them when the weaving is finished.

Let's Talk About It

Making brooms is an old art form that has almost been forgotten. Ages ago, broom makers developed techniques to create brooms for every different household task.

What other materials might they have used in making brooms?

What acted as a loom in this project?

What was the weft, warp, and shuttle?

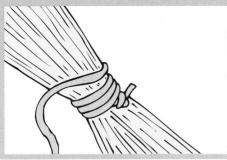

steps 1 & 2

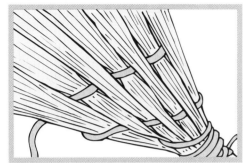

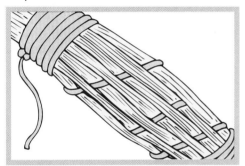

step 3

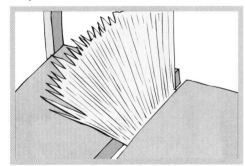

step 4

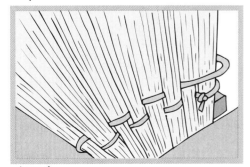

step 5

Steps to Follow

1 Gather a bundle of broom straw. Tap the straw on the table to get one end of the bundle flat and even. Use the 30" (76 cm) piece of twine and tie it 5" (13 cm) from the flat end. Tie the straw together with a square knot. (See page 45.)

2 Now wrap the twine four times around the bundle of straw. As you wrap, move back toward the flat end. This is the beginning of the broom handle.

3 Separate the handle into seven clusters and begin the weaving. Wrap the twine over and under the clusters of straw. Work back toward the end of the handle.

4 Approximately 2" (5 cm) from the end, wrap the twine around the handle four times and make a knot. Leave enough twine for a loop to hang the broom.

5 Flatten the broom end between two chairs. Use fingers to separate the broom into five sections.

6 Weave the 24" (61 cm) piece of twine in and out between the clusters. Weave the twine several times across the broom. Tie a knot to hold the twine in place. Children may add a second row of weaving to add extra strength to the broom.

7 Trim the broom end with garden shears or scissors.

step 6

How to Braid

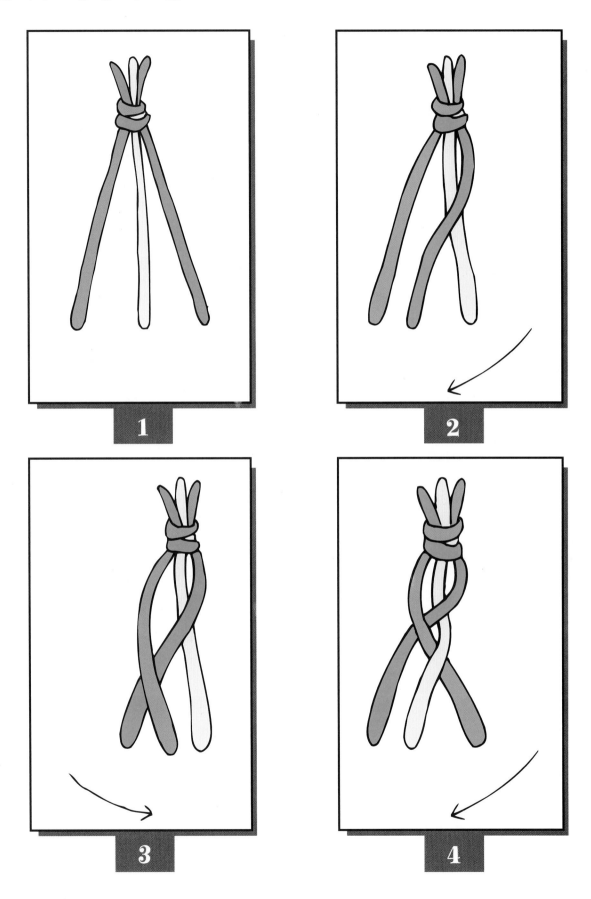

ArtWorks for Kids • EMC 761

How to Tie a Square Knot

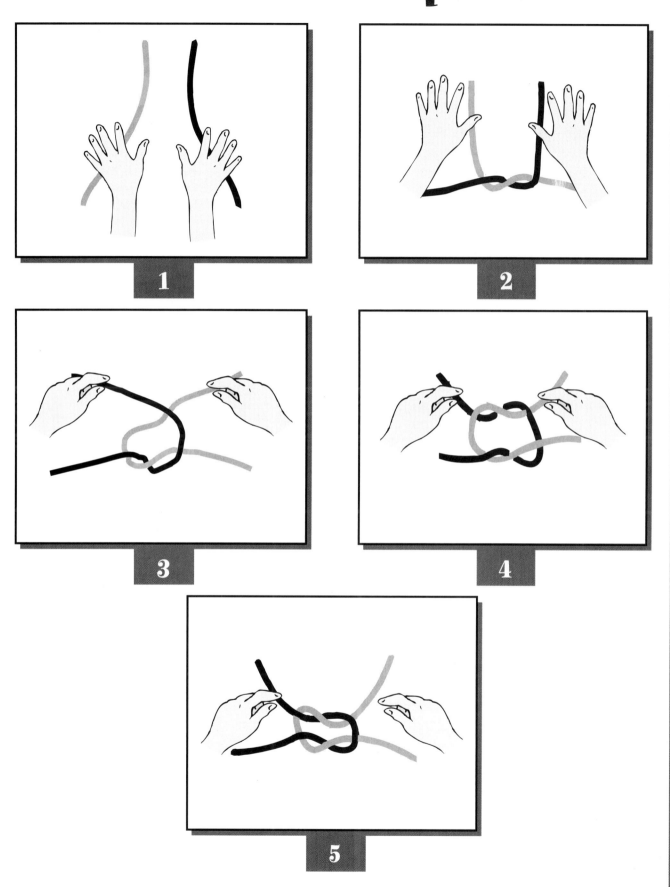

Parts of the Loom

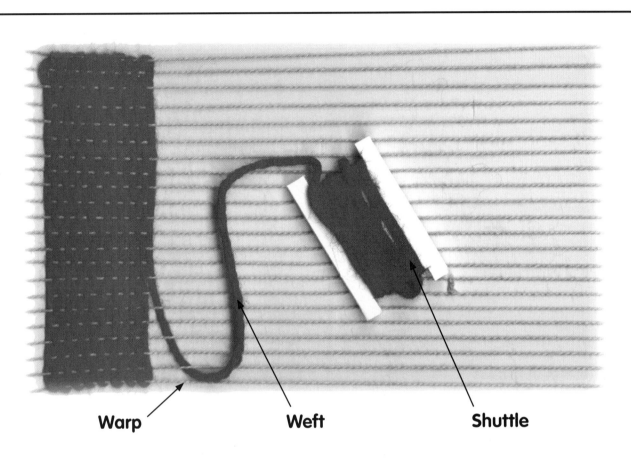

Warp   **Weft**   **Shuttle**

Warp lines are threaded onto a loom.

Weft threads are wound onto a shuttle.

The **shuttle** passes over and under between the warp lines, creating the woven surface.

Basic Weave Patterns

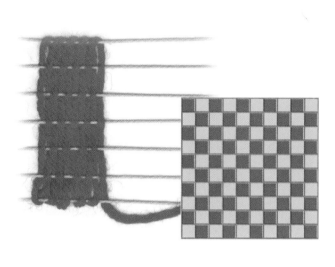

Regular Weave

An even pattern is created in a woven piece by passing the weft **over** one warp and **under** the next.

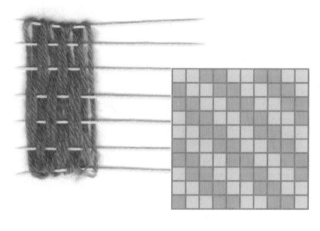

Twill Weave

A diagonal pattern is created in a woven piece by passing the weft thread over one and under two or more warp threads.

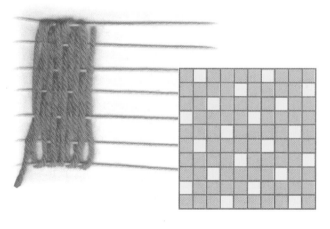

Satin Weave

A smooth surface is created in the woven piece by passing the weft thread over several warp lines at a time.

Clay

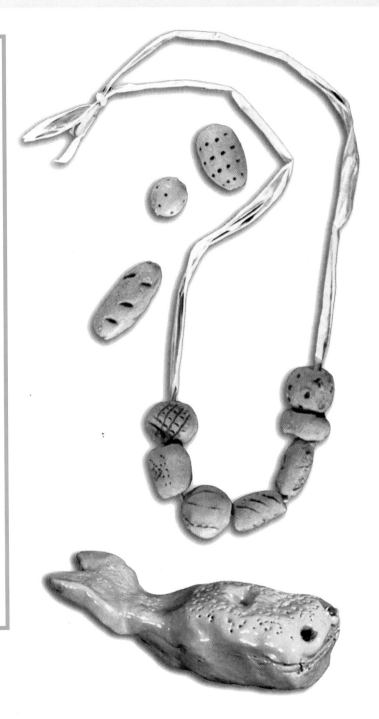

Cutting Clay

Clay usually comes in 25-lb. (11.3 kg) bags. You will need to cut, re-bag, and seal it as you do projects. If you cut off more than you need, simply place each piece in an airtight plastic bag for future use.

Always store your clay in a cool, dry place. Any scraps can be put in a bucket with water for future use.

Use a wire or fishing line to make cutting clay easier. Do not use a knife. If you are teaching a large class, cut your clay in advance. Up to one-half hour before class time is fine. Cut, separate, and lay the clay on a tray or some sturdy surface and cover it with wet paper towels. Clay starts to dry as soon as air hits it. To cut down on drying and cracking, keep it covered with damp cloths when not in use.

Excessive handling of clay can also cause drying.

Clay Colors

Using different colors of clay adds variety.

- Terra-cotta clay creates rich-looking finished projects even without glaze. It is also the most economical to use.
- White clays are good if the project needs to be light in color or will have a white or light-color glaze. This clay tends to be the most expensive.
- Black clay is rare but exquisite when fired and polished.
- Gray clay is more common and has a fine texture.
- Green and blue clays can be interesting for special projects.

Ten Tips on Using Clay

1 Have all the materials ready before starting. Suddenly remembering you need to put on an apron is unsettling once your hands are covered with clay.

2 Check clay for air bubbles. Air pockets can expand in the kiln and blow up your project. If air bubbles are present, wedge the clay for at least five minutes. Wedge by using the palm of your hands to lightly press down, much like kneading bread. Never poke fingers into the clay or flatten and fold it over. This is a sure way to cause air bubbles.

3 Try using a rolling pin or a dowel rod (roller) to roll out clay. To ensure uniform thickness, place two boards of the desired thickness on either side of the clay before rolling it out.

4 Make slip before starting a project that requires pieces to be attached. Slip is clay dissolved in water to the consistency of cake batter. Never use plain water to attach pieces. Slip acts like glue to hold layers of clay together.

5 Use water to moisten clay if cracking occurs. Be careful not to use too much, as it will take longer for the project to dry.

6 Use a sponge dipped in water to smooth lumps and cracking.

7 Place cardboard covered with a piece of clean paper (not newspaper) on the work surface. When the project is finished, you can peel the paper off easily. If you work directly on the cardboard, your project may stick to it. The cardboard acts as a tray when a project needs to be moved.

8 When you attach pieces to each other, always score both parts and use slip.

9 Always make sure the piece is completely dry before putting it in the kiln. If it is cold to the touch, it still has moisture in it and will blow up if fired. The piece will feel warm when completely dry.

10 If a project is to hold food that is not wrapped, such as soup, a drink, etc., check the glazes to make sure they are nontoxic and have no lead.

Types of Pottery

There are many types of pottery:

Pinch Pots

Pinch pots seem to be the easiest for young children or those who have never crafted with clay before, since absolutely nothing can go wrong.

Coil Pots

Coil pots are a favorite as they can be any shape you desire and most children love to make the long snake-like coils.

Slab Pots

Slab pots are equally easy but look quite different from pinch or coil pottery.

Hand-thrown Pots

Hand-thrown pots are shaped on a potter's wheel with the hands and water while the wheel is spinning. Many ceramic and pottery classes are held at local community centers or city colleges that teach this technique.

Faux Fossils

Create fossil look-alikes while learning the techniques of working with clay.

Vocabulary

faux

fixative

fossil

kiln

Materials

- clay
- newspaper
- cardboard with clean paper cover
- rolling pin
- shells, leaves, flowers, plastic fish, etc.
- magnets (optional)
- spray fixative (optional)
- access to a kiln

Project Notes

- For easy cleanup, cover the work surface with newspaper. Always work the project on a piece of cardboard with a clean paper cover.
- Don't be concerned about the shape of the fossils.
- Glue a magnet on the back to make a unique refrigerator magnet.

Let's Talk About It

How are real fossils created?

How is this clay different from clays made of plastic?

Steps to Follow

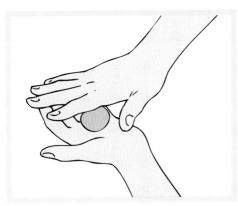

step 2

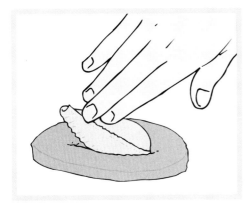

step 3

1 Cut a block of clay for each child. Make it large enough to make several fossils.

2 Pinch off a piece of clay. Roll the clay flat with a rolling pin or a roller to approximately 1/2" (1.25 cm) thick. It may be an irregular shape.

3 Place a shell or other object you want to imprint on top of the clay. Press down gently with your hand or with a roller.

4 Lift the object to see if the impression is deep enough.

5 Let the clay dry thoroughly and fire it in a kiln.

6 Instead of glazing the "fossils," spray them with a fixative to preserve them. An adult should spray the projects in a well-ventilated area.

How to use a rolling pin or roller with clay

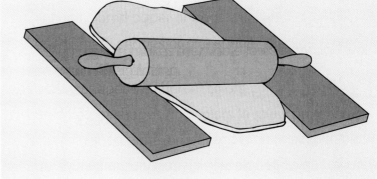

ArtWorks for Kids • EMC 761

Making Beads

Create clay beads for use in making necklaces and costumes.

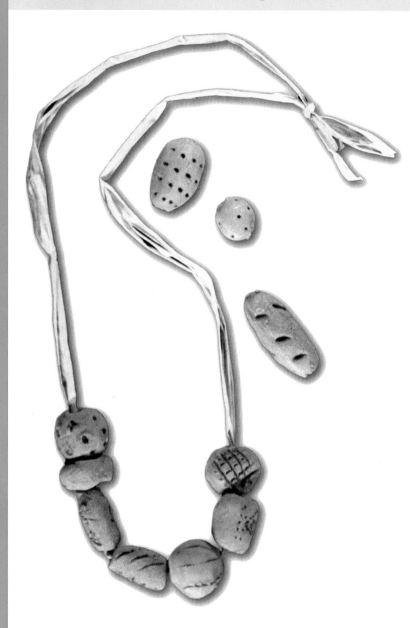

Vocabulary

glaze

texture

Materials

- clay
- newspaper
- cardboard with clean paper cover
- rolling pin
- toothpicks
- cords for stringing beads
- glazes or paints
- spray fixative (optional)
- access to a kiln

Project Notes

- Set up a work area with newspaper and a suitable cardboard work surface.
- Clay shrinks while drying, so make sure the hole in each bead is large enough to fit the cord or string that it will be strung on.

Let's Talk About It

Describe the way clay feels in your hands. Does it feel cold, elastic, wet, or dry?

Why do you think people still like to sculpt with clay?

How is sculpting with clay like painting a picture?

Steps to Follow

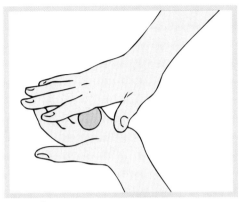
step 2

1 Cut a block of clay for each child. Make it large enough to make up to a dozen beads.

2 Pinch off small pieces of clay and roll between the palms of the hands. Create the desired shape: round, oblong, oval, or square.

3 Roll the piece over a textured cloth or use a toothpick to create a design. Keep the designs simple.

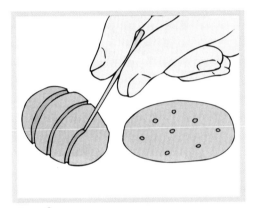
step 3

4 Make a hole through the bead with a toothpick. Allow for shrinkage of the clay as it dries.

5 Dry the beads and fire them.

step 4

Finishing touches

• Beads created from terra-cotta clay are attractive with only a spray fixative used as a sealer.

• If a glaze is used, be sure to elevate the beads in the kiln so they do not stick to the shelf.

• Finishing with tempera paint creates a primitive look, and the beads will wear well if sprayed with a fixative.

     ArtWorks for Kids • EMC 761

Pinch Pots

Create pottery using a pinching and pulling method.

Let's Talk About It

Clay is very elastic. How does this help in making a pinch pot?

What other things besides pots could be created with this method?

Vocabulary

paddling

pinching

pottery

pulling

Materials

- clay
- newspaper
- cardboard with clean paper cover
- cup of water
- sponge
- wooden spoon
- texturing tools: forks, shells, burlap
- access to a kiln

Project Notes

- Model the process of making a pinch pot for your children before they begin. This will give you an opportunity to point out the techniques and possible pitfalls of the process.

- It is easy to weaken the walls of the pot by making them too thin. About 1/4" (0.6 cm) is a good thickness.

Steps to Follow

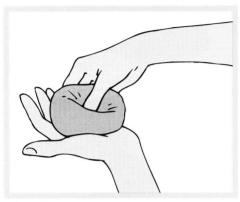

step 2

step 3

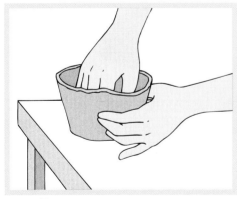

step 5

1 Cut a piece of clay the size of a tennis ball for each child. Using hands and a flat surface, round the clay into a smooth ball shape.

2 Holding the ball in one palm, start pinching a pocket in the center with the thumb and fingers of the other hand. Don't let the walls get too thin. Work the pot slowly by pinching and pulling.

3 Smooth away any fingerprints with a wooden spoon. Place the pot over one fist and gently slap it with the flat surface of the spoon. This process of smoothing out the lumps and fingerprints is called paddling.

4 The top edge of the pot will be irregular. You may trim it with a knife or leave it uneven to add character.

5 Set the pot on a flat surface that is covered with clean paper. Gently press down to form the base. This will keep the finished pot from rocking.

6 Add texture to pots with tools such as forks, shells, or burlap. Press into the outer walls to leave an impression. If any cracking should appear, use water and a sponge to smooth out the clay.

7 After the pot is completely dry, place it in a kiln to fire. Glaze and fire again. If glazes are not available, try painting with tempera and finishing with a spray fixative.

Coil Pots

Create pottery using coils of clay.

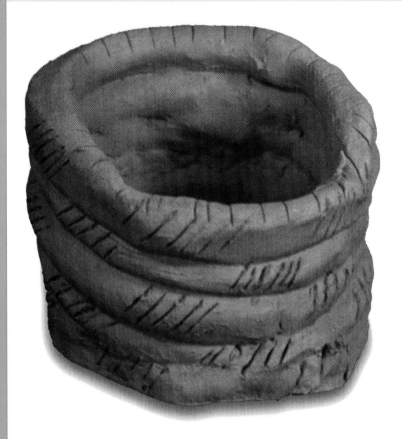

Vocabulary

coil   slip

score   smooth

Materials

- clay
- newspaper
- cardboard with clean paper cover
- cup of water
- plastic knife
- texturing tools
- rolling pin
- slip (see page 50, tip 4)
- glaze (optional)
- craft stick
- smooth stone
- access to a kiln

Let's Talk About It

How is the clay different when fired rather than air dried?

How is a coil pot different from a pinch pot?

Do we think about form and design while creating a pot as we do when painting a picture?

Project Notes

- Model the process of making a coil pot before children begin. This is an opportunity to point out techniques and possible pitfalls of the process.

- If the pots are to be glazed and are designed to hold food, remember to use nontoxic glazes.

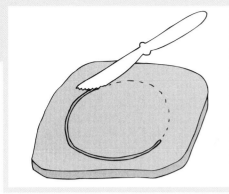

step 2

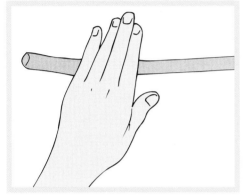

step 3

step 4

step 6

Steps to Follow

1 Start with a block of clay approximately 1 1/4 lb. (114 g). Pinch off a piece the size of a golf ball to form the base of the pot. Flatten this piece of clay with a roller to 1/4" (0.6 cm) in thickness.

2 Decide on a shape for the base and cut out the shape with the plastic knife. Place it on the paper-covered cardboard. Use this paper to turn the project while working.

3 Pinch off another golf ball-size piece of clay. Squeeze it into a rope. Roll it from the center toward the ends until it is a coil about the size of a finger. If the clay becomes dry, add a bit of water.

4 Moisten the base, score the surface with the knife, and add a layer of slip. Lift the coil carefully so it doesn't stretch, and place it on the base. Use a craft stick in a wiping motion to make the coil adhere to the base permanently.

5 Continue to add coils on top of the first coil. With each new coil, the previous surface must be scored and layered with slip. To make the pot wider, place each new coil to the outside of the previous one. To make the walls contract, place each coil to the inside of the previous one.

6 After several coils are in place, support the outside wall with one hand and use a smooth stone dipped in water to smooth the inside. Then smooth the outside wall.

7 After all the coils are in place and the entire surface is smoothed, add decorations with texturing tools. Dry the pottery thoroughly and fire it. Glaze the pot (optional) and then fire it again.

Hanging Slab Vase

Create a vase starting with a flat piece or slab of clay.

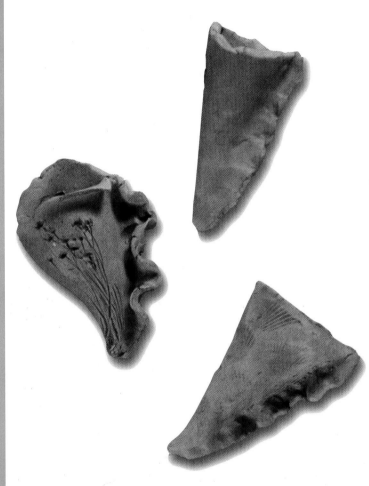

Vocabulary

cornucopia

score

slab

slip

Materials

- clay
- newspaper
- cardboard with clean paper cover
- cup of water
- plastic knife
- texturing tools: nails, pencils, orange sticks, etc.
- sponge
- burlap or other textured fabric
- rolling pin
- slip
- access to a kiln

Let's Talk About It

How is making a slab pot different from making a pinch or coil pot?

What types of materials from nature could be used to decorate the slab pot?

Project Notes

- Model the process of making a slab pot before children begin. This will give you an opportunity to point out techniques and possible pitfalls of the process.
- Moisten clay periodically with the sponge and water to prevent cracking.
- Fill the finished vase with dried flowers or leaves.

Steps to Follow

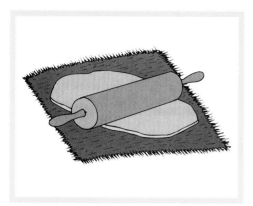

steps 1 & 2

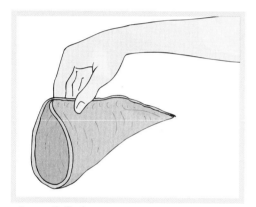

steps 3 & 4

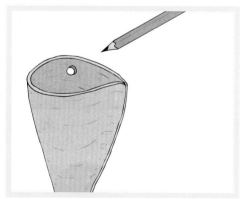

step 5

1 Cut a block of clay the size of a tennis ball. To prevent cracking, moisten the clay with a sponge and water before starting.

2 Place the clay on a piece of burlap or other fabric with a coarse texture. Use a rolling pin to flatten the clay to 1/4" (0.6 cm) thick. Leave the edges uneven or trim with a plastic knife.

3 Peel the clay from the fabric and roll it cornucopia style. Be careful not to damage the texture.

4 With a knife, score the edges where the clay overlaps and add slip to act as glue. Gently press or pinch the edges together to seal.

5 Punch a hole with a pencil approximately 1/2" (1.25 cm) from the top so the pot can be hung on a wall.

6 Place the vase on a clean sheet of paper and let it dry completely. Fire the pot in the kiln.

7 Glaze the pot inside and out and fire it again.

Basic Tiles

Learn to make a basic tile using a slab technique.

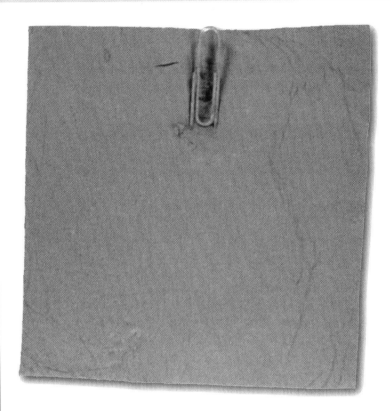

Let's Talk About It

What are some uses for clay tiles?

Where might you see clay tiles in your home and community?

How is making tiles similar to making slab pots?

Vocabulary

slab   texture

template   tile

Materials

- clay
- newspaper
- cardboard with clean paper cover
- rolling pin
- paper clips (optional)
- plastic knife
- texturing tools
- 5" (13 cm) square templates made from tagboard
- glaze (optional)

Project Notes

- Model the process of making a tile before children begin. Use this time to refer to the tips listed on page 50. These reminders can make the difference between a successful experience and a disaster.

- It is important to work on cardboard with a clean paper cover. This surface keeps the tile from sticking to the work area and allows the clay to be picked up without distorting the shape.

ArtWorks for Kids • EMC 761

Steps to Follow

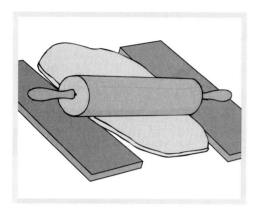
step 1

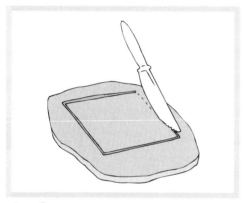
step 2

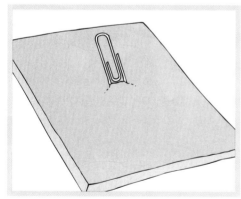
step 3

1 Cut a piece of clay. Place the clay on the cardboard covered with clean paper. Using the rolling pin, flatten the clay starting from the middle and working out toward the edges until the slab is about 1/4" (0.6 cm) thick.

2 Place the template on the clay and roll over it with the rolling pin to leave a slight impression. Use the knife to cut around the template edges. Remove the scraps and save them for future use. Remove the template. Now the basic clay tile has been created.

3 Insert a paper clip hanger if the tile is to be hung on the wall. Insert it toward the top of the tile at an angle with the loop sticking out. Be careful not to push it through the tile.

4 Pick up the paper the tile is on and flip it over, clip side down, onto a clean paper. Peel the paper off the tile.

5 Decorate the tile with texturing tools. Let it dry and fire it in the kiln. Children may choose to glaze the textured tile. Then the tile will have to be fired again.

Suggested texturing techniques
- cross-hatching with a fork
- impressions of leaves or feathers
- impressions of pasta letter forms to create words
- pictures drawn with toothpicks

         ArtWorks for Kids • EMC 761

Nature Tiles

Create a textured tile using the slab technique and items collected from nature.

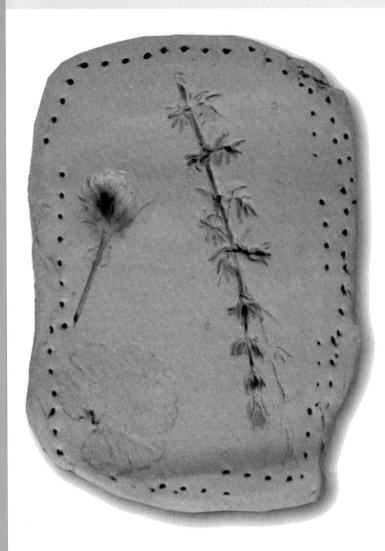

Vocabulary

impression   tile

imprint

Materials

- clay
- newspaper
- cardboard with clean paper cover
- rolling pin
- plastic knife
- templates made from tagboard
- fresh flowers, leaves, etc.
- paper clips
- tempera paints
- spray fixative (optional)
- access to a kiln

Let's Talk About It

How is imprinting in clay similar to printing with paint on paper? How is it different?

Can you see and feel how the texture of the clay changes when the objects are imprinted?

Project Notes

- Before beginning the project, review the procedure for making a basic tile on page 63 and the tips on page 50.
- Do this as part of science or ecology lessons. Children can collect their own materials for imprinting tiles.
- This tile is good to use as a coaster or trivet. It would make a nice holiday gift for parents.
- Do not glaze these tiles—it will ruin the impressions. Instead, paint with tempera paint and spray with a fixative.

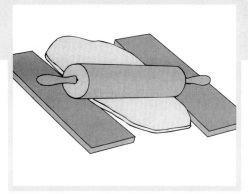

step 1

step 1

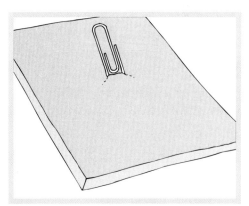

step 2

step 4

Steps to Follow

1 Start by making a basic tile. (See page 63 for details.) Roll out a chunk of clay. Choose a template shape and place it on the clay. Gently roll over it to leave an impression on the clay. Then cut out the shape with a plastic knife.

2 Insert a paper clip toward the top edge of the tile if it is to be hung up. Flip the tile over.

3 Choose a fresh flower or leaf to imprint. Make sure it has good detail so the imprint will not disappear when the clay dries.

4 Place the object or objects on the tile and gently but firmly press with the rolling pin. Be sure to get a clear impression before removing the objects.

5 Gently remove the objects from the clay impression. Set the tiles aside to dry.

6 Fire the tiles in the kiln.

7 Tiles may be left in their natural state or painted with tempera paint. If painted, spray the tiles with fixative.

Picture Frame Tiles

Create a frame from a slab of clay. Add a textured design using a variety of tools.

Vocabulary

slab

template

texture

Materials

- clay
- newspaper
- cardboard with clean paper cover
- rolling pin
- plastic knife
- templates cut from tagboard
- paper clips
- small photos
- glue
- texturing tools: pencils, craft sticks, nails, toothpicks, etc.
- access to a kiln

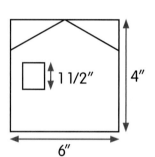

Let's Talk About It

How does crafting with clay resemble weaving?

How are printing and clay crafting similar and how are they different?

Project Notes

- Review the steps for making a tile plus the helpful tips on page 50.
- Glazing these projects tends to obscure the textured design. Tempera paint and fixative may be a wiser choice if color is desired.

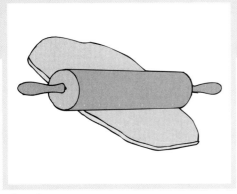

step 1

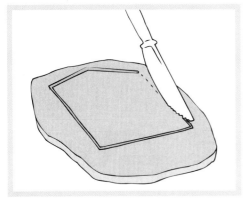

step 2

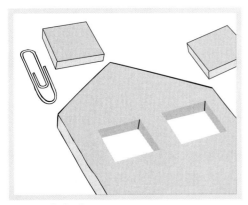

steps 3 & 4

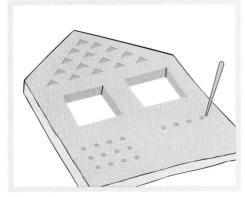

step 5

Steps to Follow

1 Make a basic tile. Place a chunk of clay on the cardboard. Using the rolling pin, flatten the clay starting from the middle and working out toward the edges until the slab is about 1/4" (0.6 cm) thick.

2 Choose a template such as a rectangle or square for the shape of the frame—perhaps the shape of a house or schoolhouse. Place the template over the tile and make an imprint using the rolling pin. Cut away scraps and save for later use.

3 Cut a rectangular template for the inside of the frame. Make an imprint of this template on the clay with the rolling pin. Cut out the rectangles with the plastic knife and remove them.

4 Insert a paper clip hanger if the tile is to be hung on the wall. Insert it toward the top at an angle with the loop sticking out. Be careful not to push it through the tile. Flip the tile over.

5 Using texturing tools, add designs to the frame. Craft sticks, toothpicks, shells, etc., can be used to make wonderful textures.

6 Dry the tile thoroughly and fire it. If desired, add color with tempera paint and spray with a fixative. These frames are also very effective left with the natural finish.

7 When the frame is finished, attach the pictures to the back of the frame with glue.

Whales

Create an animal sculpture using the basic pull-out method of sculpting.

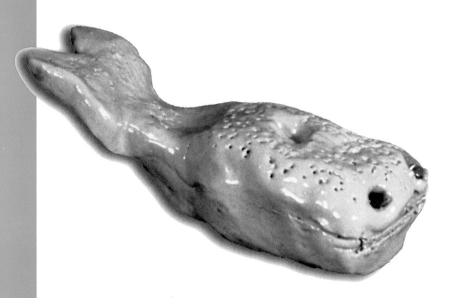

Vocabulary

glaze

sculpture

Materials

- clay
- newspaper
- cardboard with clean paper cover
- cup of water
- craft stick
- toothpick
- access to a kiln

Let's Talk About It

What kinds of materials can be used for sculptures other than clay?

How did pulling the tail of the whale up or down suggest movement?

How do you think sculpting animals with clay started?

Project Notes

- Experiment to see what kind of effects can be created with clay before doing a finished sculpture. Do not use the experimental clay to do the finished project. Air will have been trapped in the clay, which will cause problems during firing.

Origins of clay

Building with clay predates recorded history. Pottery and clay sculptures can be found in cultures throughout the world.

Steps to Follow

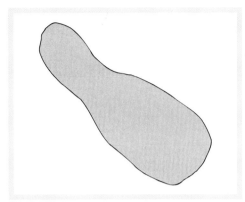

step 2

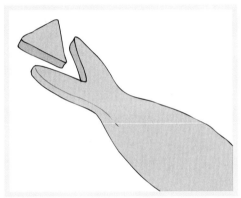

step 3

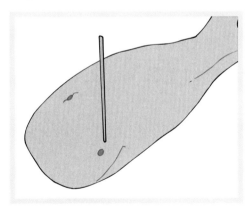

step 4

1 Cut clay to the size of a stick of butter. Gently roll and mold the clay until it looks somewhat like a potato.

2 About a third of the way from the end of the clay "potato," pull out a tail portion by gently squeezing your fingers around the piece of clay. Leave the majority of the clay for the head and body of the whale.

3 Flatten the tail area with your fingers. Don't make it too thin. Use a craft stick to cut V-shaped flukes at the end of the tail. You may want to pull out fins on both sides of the body.

4 Make eyes and a blow hole by gently pushing a toothpick in and out. Use the same toothpick to carve out a mouth. Also carve the artist's initials on the bottom.

5 At this point you can suggest movement by bending the tail up or down.

6 Poke two holes with a pencil in the underside of the thickest part of the whale body to aid the drying process. Dry the whale thoroughly and then fire it in a kiln.

7 Adding a glaze makes the whale look shiny and wet. Fire again after glazing.

Bears

Create a more sophisticated animal sculpture using a basic pull-out method of sculpting.

Vocabulary

pull-out method

Materials

- clay
- newspaper
- cardboard with clean paper cover
- craft stick
- toothpick
- cup of water
- plastic fork or comb
- access to a kiln

Let's Talk About It

Why is balance important when doing a sculpture?

How did you create texture in your sculpture?

Project Notes

- As the bear is being sculpted, remember that it needs to stand up on four legs. However, if the bear is "unsteady" on its feet, you can always have it sit down.

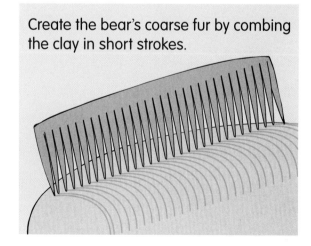

Create the bear's coarse fur by combing the clay in short strokes.

 ArtWorks for Kids • EMC 761

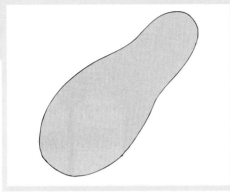

step 1

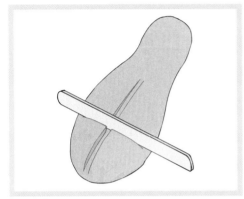

step 2

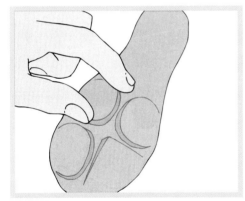

step 3

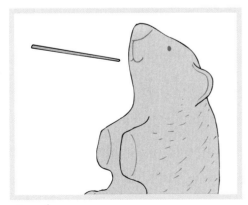

step 4

Steps to Follow

1 Cut the clay to about the size of two sticks of butter. Roll and pat the rectangular block into a potato shape. Using about a third of the potato shape, gently pull out a head portion. Do not squeeze too hard. Bears have thick necks.

2 Turn the bear over on its back. Using a craft stick, mark lines for the legs.

3 Form the leg sections by gently pulling and pushing the clay into rounded legs. Keep the legs short and thick. Bears do not have long, thin legs.

4 Look at the head portion. Form the nose so it is slightly pointed. Use your thumb and forefinger to gently pinch out two ears. They should be rounded, set apart, and not too thin. Use a toothpick to make eyes. Draw a line around the nose for definition.

5 Use a fork or comb to create texture for the fur by combing the clay with short strokes. Decide whether your bear will stand on all fours, sit down, or lie down.

6 Poke two holes in the underside of the bear with a pencil to aid in drying. Fire the sculpture in the kiln.

7 Glazing is optional. If you are using a terra-cotta clay, the final product is very attractive without glaze.

ArtWorks for Kids • EMC 761

Fantasy Fish

Create a fantasy fish sculpture while learning the add-on method of sculpting.

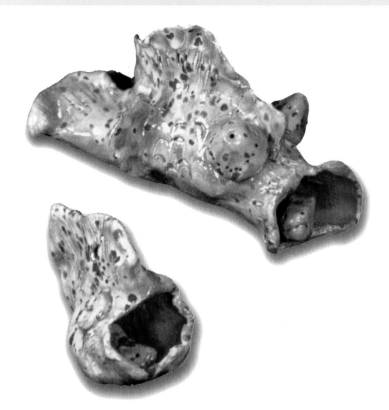

Let's Talk About It

How is the add-on method of sculpting different from the pull-out method?

How can using paper aid in creating different effects in sculpting?

Vocabulary

add-on
kiln
scoring
slip

Materials

- clay
- newspaper
- cardboard with clean paper cover
- rolling pin
- cup of water
- cup of slip (see page 50, tip 4)
- plastic knife
- texturing tools
- toothpicks
- small pieces of crumpled newspaper
- access to a kiln

Project Notes

- Because this clay will be rolled out (eliminating air pockets), leftover clay may be used.
- If fish are to be used as ornaments for your aquarium, be sure to use nontoxic glazes.

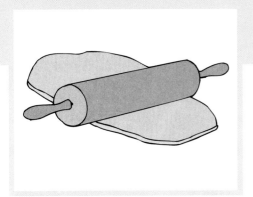

step 1

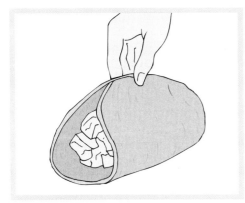

steps 2 & 3

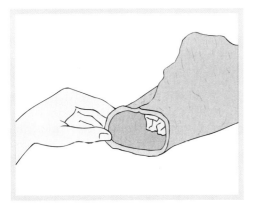

step 4

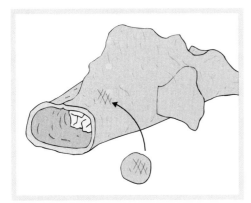

step 5

Steps to Follow

1 Start with a piece of clay about the size of an orange. Use a rolling pin to flatten the clay. Start rolling out from the middle until it is about 1/2" (1.25 cm) to 1/4" (0.6 cm) thick. Edges should not be uniform.

2 Place a tightly crumpled piece of newspaper in the center of the clay slab. This will act as a form for the body of the fish.

3 Score the edges of the clay slab with a knife and add slip for glue. Pull up the two sides of the clay and pinch it together. This forms the top back of the fish.

4 Pinch the tail area together at one end of the fish. Pull and pinch the other end to form the head and open mouth. Don't worry about trapping the newspaper inside the fish. It will burn up when the clay is fired.

5 Create eyes by rolling small balls of clay in the palms. Score the back of the eyes and the eye area on the fish head. Using slip for glue, firmly set the eyes in place. Fins may also be added following this same procedure.

6 Allow the fish to dry thoroughly and then fire in the kiln.

7 Paint these fish with brightly colored glazes and fire again.

ArtWorks for Kids • EMC 761

Making Faces

Create a basic clay mask using slab, pull-out, and add-on techniques.

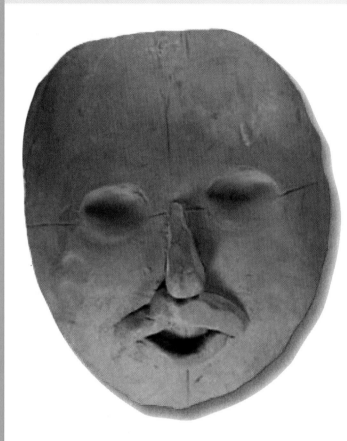

Vocabulary

add-on   mold   pull-out   slab

Materials

* clay
* crumpled newspaper
* cardboard with clean paper cover
* plastic spoon
* cup of slip
* cup of water
* pencil
* rolling pin
* access to a kiln

Let's Talk About It

Name all the different methods of clay crafting used in this project.

How did you show feeling when developing the mouth and eyes?

Project Notes

* How to place features on a face:

  Draw a vertical line down the center of the face.

  Draw a horizontal line across the face to mark the level of the eyes.

  Mark the center of the eyes at about one-third the distance between the center and sides of the face.

  Put the nose halfway between the eyes and mouth.

  Put the mouth between the nose and chin.

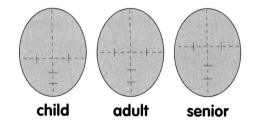

child   **adult**   **senior**

ArtWorks for Kids • EMC 761

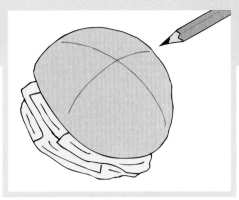

steps 1 & 2

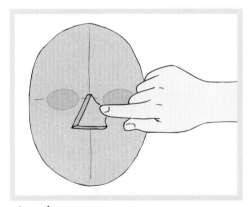

step 3

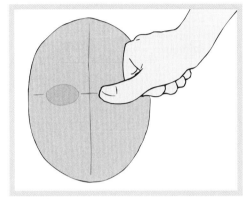

step 4

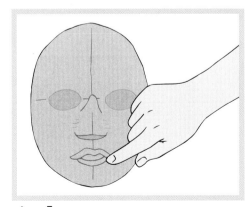

step 5

Steps to Follow

1 Start with a slab of clay approximately 1 1/2 lb. (227 g). Cut approximately 1/2" (1.25 cm) off the slab and set aside. This extra piece will be used for the nose, eyebrows, etc. Use your hands to carefully round the corners and flatten to an oval shape. Clay should be about 1/2" (1.25 cm) thick. Trim the edges of the oval to make it even.

2 Place the slab over crumpled newspaper. This will act as a mold. Ease the clay into a convex shape. If you want to hang the mask, make two holes in the top half, a finger width away from each side. Use a pencil to lightly draw placement lines on the face. (See notes on page 74.)

3 Use a spoon or your thumb to shape the eyes. Gently press in the eye shape on each side, being careful to make them even.

4 To make the nose, select a piece of the clay you set aside, and cut a pyramid shape with your knife. Score, apply slip to the edges, and join to the face. Smooth out the line around the nose with water. Shape the nose the way you like, using the pull-out method.

5 To make lips, roll a clay coil and attach it to the mouth area by scoring and using slip. Shape the mouth into a smile or a frown.

6 If desired, give the mask character by adding eyeballs, hair, eyebrows, or whiskers.

7 Dry the mask thoroughly on the mold. Then remove the mold and fire the mask. If you glaze the mask, fire it once again.

ArtWorks for Kids • EMC 761

Clay Otters

Create a clay sculpture while learning the basic pull-out method.

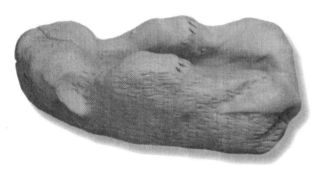

Vocabulary

clay

firing

kiln

sculpture

Materials

- clay (terra-cotta is best)
- wire clay cutter or piece of string
- cups with water
- toothpicks
- small shells
- newspapers
- cardboard with clean paper cover
- access to a kiln

Let's Talk About It

How does the clay feel and smell?

What can be used to add texture when working with clay?

Where does clay come from?

Project Notes

- Prepare a newspaper-covered area for working with the clay.
- Let children work on pieces of cardboard covered with clean paper. The project will not stick to the paper, and it can be easily transported.
- Designate a table for drying projects.
- A kiln will be used to fire this project. If a kiln is not available, use an air-dry clay.
- Use pictures of otters for reference.

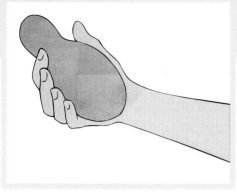

steps 1 & 2

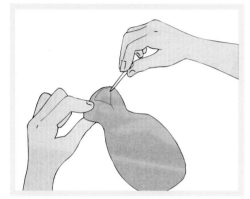

step 3

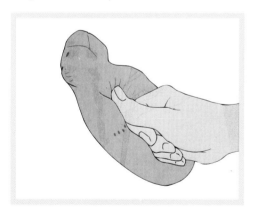

step 4

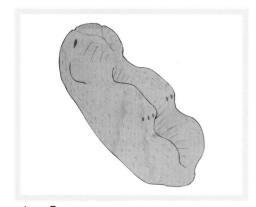

step 5

Steps to Follow

1 Cut the clay to about the size of two sticks of butter. Roll and pat the rectangular block into a potato shape.

2 Gently squeeze a third of the potato shape with the thumb and finger to form the head and neck. Pull out the basic head shape. Never tear pieces from the clay and try to reattach them. This will cause air pockets that could explode during firing.

3 Using the fingers, gently pull out two tiny ears near the neck. Don't make them too thin.

Shape the nose area. Look at a picture of a sea otter for reference. Keep the nose rounded.

Use a toothpick to draw eyes.

Draw a line around the nose area for definition.

4 The otter will be lying on its back as it does in the water. Using the thumb, gently press into the tummy area to form a shallow pocket.

Use the toothpick to draw little folded paws around the tummy area.

5 Create texture with a toothpick—make the clay look like fur by gently scratching over the back and head areas.

6 Let the finished project dry for about two weeks. Clay is dry when it is warm to the touch. Fire the otters in a kiln.

Finally, place a tiny shell on the otter's tummy.

Firing Clay

1   There are some clays on the market that are **not** intended for kiln drying. Read the labels carefully.

2   Before firing, be sure the project is dry. Cool to the touch means the clay still holds moisture. Wait until the clay feels warm or it may explode in the kiln.

3   Remember that dry clay is very fragile. One bump can cause you to be left with dust. This is one reason why it is better to fire your project rather than just let it air dry.

4   Follow kiln loading instructions. Use shelves and posts in the kiln to stack projects. Glazed projects should never touch each other or sit directly on the shelves. Use stilts to keep the glaze from melting onto the shelves. You can create several shelves full of projects.

5   A kiln works by gradually raising the temperature to bake the project. The slow rise in temperature gives the clay time to shrink and harden as the moisture evaporates.

     The temperature of a kiln rises to approximately 2,000 degrees Fahrenheit (756 degrees Celsius). Let projects cool overnight and use gloves to remove them. Removing pieces before they are cool can cause cracking.

6   If your school does not have a kiln, you may be able to find a local community college or ceramic shop that will fire the pieces for a small fee.

Air-Dry Clay

If a kiln is not available, be sure to use a clay not intended for kiln drying. Air-dry clay must never be put in a kiln and should not be glazed.

Printing

Butterfly Prints

Create an abstract design with tempera paint without using a brush.

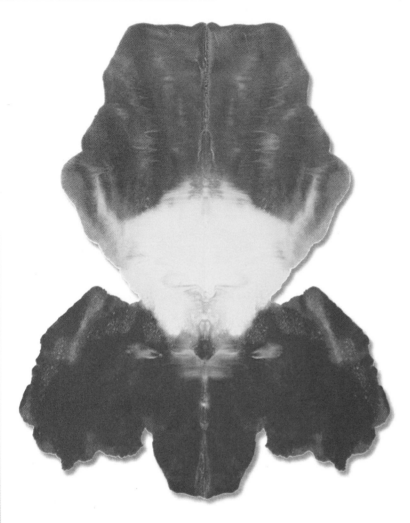

Let's Talk About It

What is the difference between printing and painting?

What are primary colors?

What are secondary colors?

Vocabulary

primary colors

printing

secondary colors

symmetrical

Materials

- plain white paper
  12" x 18" (30.5 x 46 cm)

- tempera paints
  (primary colors in squirt bottles)

Project Notes

- This project can be a supplement to a nature studies unit or a follow-up to a favorite piece of literature about butterflies.

  Talk about butterflies and the many colors and markings they have on their wings. You may want the children to cut out the print and fold it in the center so it can flutter like a butterfly when held.

- Work with small groups of children to avoid mishaps with paint. Have younger children wear smocks.

Steps to Follow

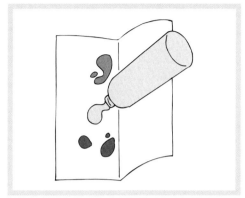

step 2

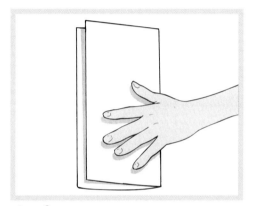

step 3

1 Fold the paper in half to a 12" x 9" (30.5 x 23 cm) size.

2 Open the paper and lay it flat on the table. Squirt a small amount of each primary color on one side of the fold. Using only a small amount of paint helps eliminate waste and speeds drying time.

3 Close the paper on the fold and press down. Encourage children to gently press over the whole paper without rubbing.

4 Open the paper to see the results of the print. Children may discover that some of the primary paint colors have mixed together to create secondary colors. Discuss why this is possible and look at the color wheel to see the relative positions of these colors.

5 Set the print aside to dry. Discuss what the children see in their print.

The color wheel

There are three **primary** colors: red, yellow, and blue. These colors can be mixed to create the **secondary** colors of orange, green, and violet. If these colors are placed in a circle showing how they are related, you have created a color wheel.

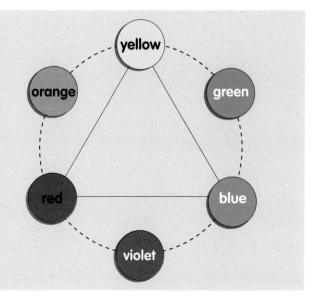

ArtWorks for Kids • EMC 761

Monoprints

A monoprint is made by pressing a sheet of paper onto a surface where paint or ink is smeared. The medium is transferred to the paper, thereby creating a print.

Let's Talk About It

What is the proper way to handle materials and to cooperate while doing a monoprint with a partner?

What are the differences between printing and painting?

Vocabulary

monoprint

printing

Materials

- plain white paper 12" x 18" (30.5 x 46 cm)
- tempera paint (various colors)
- paintbrush for each color
- masking tape
- paper towels for cleanup
- smooth, sealed-surface table or countertop

Project Notes

- Be sure the printing area is clean and clear of obstruction. Provide as many work areas as space permits. Adult supervision is advisable during printing.
- Children may need smocks.
- Children should work in pairs to manipulate the paper as they print. Both children should sign the print.
- The paper should not be moved once it is placed on the painted area.

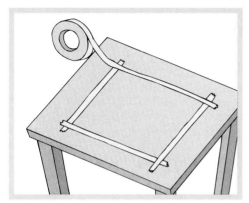

step 1

step 2

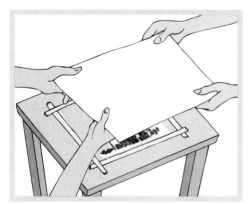

step 4

Steps to Follow

1 Mask off a 12" x 18" (30.5 x 46 cm) area on a smooth table surface.

2 Using tempera paint and brushes, paint a picture within this area.

3 Have each child choose a partner to help make a print of this tabletop painting.

4 The partners lift opposite sides of the paper and gently lay it over the top of the painting on the table. Then they gently press down over the entire paper without rubbing.

5 Lift the paper to see that the paint has transferred to the underside of the paper. Set the print aside to dry.

6 Clean off the table and prepare for the next pair of children.

Cookie Cutter Prints

Cookie cutter prints can be used to create seasonal designs for bag decorations, placemats, bulletin board backgrounds, or wrapping paper.

Vocabulary

complementary colors

patterning

printing

Materials

- paper bags or paper
- tempera paint
- small cookie cutters
- paper plates for paint

Project Notes

- Set up a work area for small groups of children to print. Prepare a place for drying projects.
- Before beginning the printing, help children plan their design.

Let's Talk About It

Discuss the importance of design and patterning when creating a print.

Think of all the different tools with which one could print.

 ArtWorks for Kids • EMC 761

Steps to Follow

step 2

step 3

1 Encourage children to think about pattern and design options for this project.

2 Dip the cutting edge of the cookie cutter into a puddle of paint on a plate. Then press the cookie cutter on a folded bag or paper. Press the cutter down and lift; do not rub the paper with the cutter.

3 Continue printing to complete the design. Clean the cookie cutters before switching to a new color of paint.

4 Let the print dry.

Different techniques to try

- Print on white paper bags with colored paint.
- Print on colored paper or bags with white paint.
- Print different shapes or one shape using different colors.
- Overlap shapes in different colors.
- Use different shapes and colors to show patterning.
- Mount finished prints on paper of contrasting colors.
- Use shapes appropriate to specific holidays to make cards or wrapping paper.

Nature Prints

Create a printed design with items collected on a nature walk.

Vocabulary

contrasting colors

design

printing

texture

Materials

- black construction paper
  6" x 18" (15 x 46 cm)
- tempera paint
  (various colors in cups)
- paintbrush for each color
- fresh leaves, flowers, bark, etc.
- newspaper

Project Notes

- Take a nature walk on which children can collect their own printing materials.
- Set up a printing area covered with newspaper.
- Work in small groups so that materials can be shared.
- As leaves and flowers get limp, replace them with new ones.

Let's Talk About It

Why is black a good color for a background in this project?

What techniques should be used in printing to guarantee a clear print?

 ArtWorks for Kids • EMC 761

Steps to Follow

step 2

1 Give each child a 6" x 18" (15 x 46 cm) piece of black construction paper. Allow time to try out various arrangements of items from their nature collections.

2 Children will plan their color scheme. Model how to brush paint on the leaves, flowers, etc.

3 Place the painted item paint-side down on the black paper.

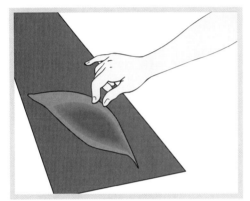

step 3

4 Place a sheet of newspaper over the black paper and press down firmly. Lift the newspaper and the leaf or flower to view the print on the black paper.

5 Continue printing the other items in the design. Encourage children to experiment with different color schemes. They will discover that contrasting colors are the most effective.

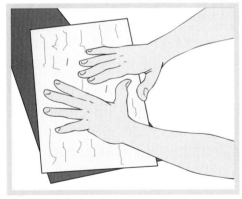

step 4

Contrasting colors

Contrast is the degree of difference between colors or tones in a piece of artwork. Using contrasting colors next to each other can help to create a point of focus. It is important to define that focus and set it apart from the background so that the picture is interesting to view. The use of black and white is the ultimate in contrasting colors.

good contrast

poor contrast

fair contrast

Bubble Prints

Create a print using, of all things, soap bubbles!

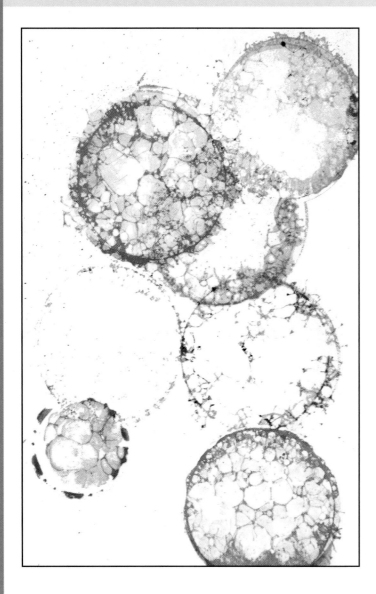

Vocabulary

primary colors

printing

secondary colors

Materials

- white paper
  9" x 12" (23 x 30.5 cm)
- water
- liquid dishwashing detergent
- tempera paint
- plastic straws
- plastic cups or bowls
- paper towels
- measuring cup

Project Notes

- Set up a workstation for small groups of children.
- Plan ahead for a place to put wet projects to dry.
- Ask an older child or an adult to blow the bubbles for younger children. For safety, use nontoxic paints and detergent.

Let's Talk About It

What are primary and secondary colors?

Why is a white paper background preferable for this type of project?

Steps to Follow

step 2

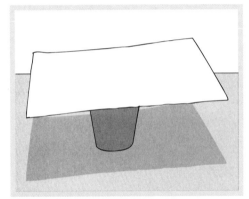

step 3

1 Children may need to experiment with this technique on a piece of scrap paper before they begin their final project. They also need to see which of the colors of paint they prefer to use in their print.

2 Place the straw in the bubble mixture and blow. Blow until bubbles extend up past the lip of the cup or bowl. Remove the straw.

3 Place a sheet of paper gently over the bubbles. Wait for the bubbles to pop.

4 Lift the paper and marvel at the result. Set the paper aside and let it dry.

5 Children may add more prints to the page and experiment with designs and color combinations. Let the prints dry in between color changes.

How to make the bubble mixture

Mix water, paint, and detergent in equal parts in cups or bowls.
Troubleshooting hints:

- If the mixture bubbles but does not go past the rim of the cup, add water.
- If the mixture does not bubble at all, add detergent.
- If the bubbles are too faint, add paint.

Soft Rubbings

Create a print using pastel chalk and a stencil. Add details of buildings, fish, plants, or animals to finish the picture.

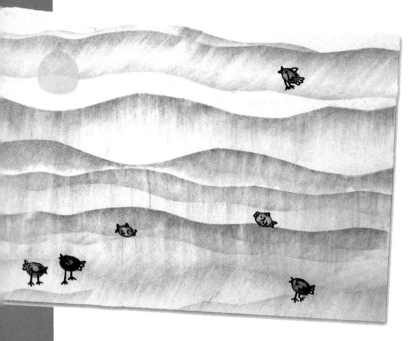

Vocabulary

color scheme   pastels

cool colors   stencil

fixative   warm colors

Materials

- white paper
  9" x 12" (23 x 30.5 cm)
- newspaper
- pastel chalks
- tagboard strips
  2" x 12" (5 x 30.5 cm)
  (4 or more per child)
- cotton balls (2 to 3 per child)
- scissors
- black fine-tip marker (1 per child)
- black ink pad
- spray fixative

Let's Talk About It

Why is the choice of color scheme important?

Why are some colors referred to as cool and others as warm?

Why is the use of a fixative necessary with this medium?

Project Notes

- Precut the stencils for younger children.
- Suggest that children can be inspired by shapes around them when cutting the stencil: the rectangular shapes of buildings or the curving shapes of mountain ranges and rippling water. Stencil cuts should be kept simple.
- Offer clean cotton balls after each color change so colors don't get mixed and muddied.
- Encourage children to plan their design and color scheme ahead of time.
- Use spray fixatives in a well-ventilated area.

Steps to Follow

1 Cut varying shapes along one long edge of each tagboard strip.

2 Lay the first stencil piece on newspaper and cover the cut edge with a layer of chalk.

3 Place that stencil in the desired spot on the white paper and hold firmly. Using a cotton ball, brush the chalk onto the paper. Lift the stencil carefully to see the design.

4 Continue this same process with the other stencil strips until the entire paper is covered. Use a new strip for each color of chalk.

5 Use the ink pad and black marker to add details of animals, trees, buildings, people, etc. Press a fingertip on the ink pad and then press the finger onto the paper. Outline and add detail to each resulting figure with the marker.

6 Spray the final project with fixative to prevent smudges.

step 1

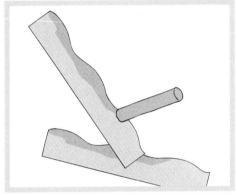

step 2

step 3

Let's talk about colors schemes

• Cool colors such as blues, purples, and greens can suggest oceans or mountains.

• Warm colors such as oranges, yellows, and reds can suggest desert landscapes or sunsets.

ArtWorks for Kids • EMC 761

Fantasy Fowl

Use materials found in nature and the classroom to make birds with colorful plumage.

Vocabulary

fantasy   printing   realistic

Materials

- various colors of tempera paint in cups
- tempera paint on paper plates
- paintbrush for each color
- paper towels
- cotton swab (one per child)
- construction paper 12" x 18" (30.5 x 46 cm)
- feathers (several per child)
- broad-tip marker

Project Notes

- Set up materials so that children can work in small groups.
- Children should wear smocks or old shirts.
- After applying paint to feathers, separate the feather parts to help keep the "feather look." Never saturate the feather with paint or the texture will be lost. Replace soggy feathers with fresh ones.
- Show paintings and photographs of realistic birds. Observe the many colors and shapes of feathers. Discuss how realistic bird paintings differ from your fantasy print.

Let's Talk About It

What other types of nature objects can be used to make prints?

How do designs change from an original idea to the finished product?

Would it be easier to paint a picture of a bird or to print one using this method?

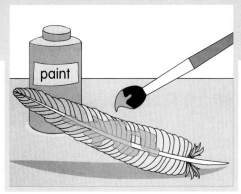

step 2

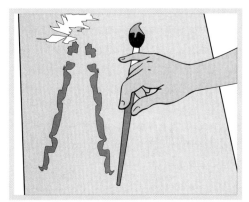

step 3

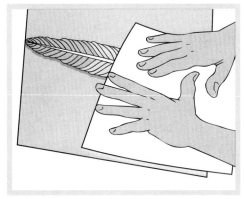

step 5

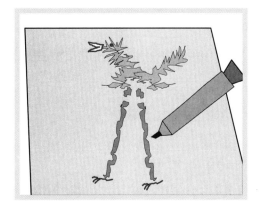

steps 6 & 7

Steps to Follow

1 Think about what this fantasy fowl will look like, then decide whether the paper will be used horizontally or vertically. Children may want to lightly pencil in a simple drawing of a bird as a guideline.

2 Paint one side of a feather and place it paint-side down on the paper. Encourage children to work from the top to the bottom of the design to avoid smudging.

3 Place a paper towel on top of the feather and press gently. Remove the towel and gently lift the feather to see the print.

4 Have children continue printing with new feathers until they have completed their bird's body. Set the paper aside to dry.

5 When prints are dry, lay a paintbrush handle down in one of the plates of tempera to coat one side. Have children use the brush handle to print legs on their bird.

6 While the legs are drying, dip a cotton swab in tempera and print the eyes.

7 After the paint is dry, use a broad-tip marker to make the feet and a beak.

 ArtWorks for Kids • EMC 761

Go Fish

Using mixed media, children create an underwater scene showing dimension and movement.

Vocabulary

background   mixed media
foreground

Materials

- white drawing paper
  9" x 12" (23 x 30.5 cm) or
  12" x 18" (30.5 x 46 cm)
- crayons
- fresh fish (small)
- black tempera paint or printer's ink
- brayer or brush
- newspaper
- cotton balls
- paper towels

Project Notes

- This project can be done by children of all ages and is a good one to do in small groups.

- Select small fish that will fit on the paper without filling the page. Choose fish that are fresh and in good shape.

- Show how objects slightly to the right or left of center make the object appear to be entering or leaving the scene.

Let's Talk About It

What is mixed media?

Does the artwork show movement and depth?

Locate foreground, middle ground, and background objects.

step 1

step 2

step 4

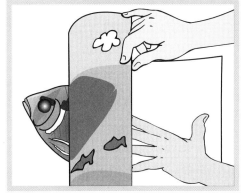

steps 5 & 6

Steps to Follow

1 Sketch an underwater scene on the paper. Color the page completely with crayon. Encourage children to fill the page with all the things one might find underwater.

2 Squeeze paint or ink onto a smooth surface. Spread it evenly with a brayer until the brayer is coated evenly with paint or ink. If a brayer and ink are not available, a brush and tempera paint may be used.

3 Blot excess moisture from the fish with a paper towel. Stuff tiny bits of cotton or paper towel under the gill and lateral fin of the fish so they will print clearly. Place the fish on a sheet of newspaper.

4 Roll or brush ink or paint over the fish, starting with the head and working toward the tail. Try not to get too much ink or paint under the scales. Lift the fish gently and place it on a clean sheet of newspaper.

5 Check the colored drawing and decide where the fish print will go. Place the drawing paper upside down on the inked fish. Starting at the center of the fish, rub gently over the paper with the fingers, moving toward the edges of the fish.

6 Gently peel the paper from the fish and let it dry.

 ArtWorks for Kids • EMC 761

String Prints

Make a string print in "relief" style. The theme may tie this project with a subject being studied in class.

Vocabulary

relief print   texture

reverse image

Materials

- string or yarn
- white glue
- heavyweight cardboard
  5" x 8" (13 x 20 cm)
- brayer
- tempera paint
- scrap paper
- construction paper
  9" x 12" (23 x 30.5 cm)
- pencil

Project Notes

- Use a good-quality string that will hold up to the wet paint.
- Keep the design simple.
- Be sure the string is securely attached to the cardboard.
- Work with small groups and monitor the amount of paint being used. The paint should completely cover the brayer in a thin, even coat.

Let's Talk About It

What is a relief print?

How does the print differ from the original design on the cardboard?

How does this string print give the impression of texture?

Steps to Follow

1 Sketch a simple design on the cardboard.

2 Put a line of glue along the design outline. Lay string along the line of glue. Fill in the design with glue and lay in string until the design is completely filled in.

3 When the design has been filled in with string, let it dry completely.

4 Squirt tempera paint on a flat surface. Roll the brayer in the tempera until it is completely coated.

5 Gently roll the coated brayer over the string design, being careful not to dislodge the string. Do not saturate the string with paint. A little paint gets the job done.

6 Place the scrap paper over the design and rub gently. Peel off the paper to view the print.

7 When children are satisfied with the print on the scrap paper, they may print the design on the construction paper. Repaint the string as needed.

steps 1 & 2

step 5

step 6

Name Chop

For thousands of years, the name chop has been the traditional way of signing a work of art in Asian countries. Here is an easy way to introduce children to this tradition.

Vocabulary

name chop

reverse print

Materials

- foam meat trays cut into 2" x 3" (5 x 8 cm) rectangles
- pencils
- tempera paint (various colors)
- paintbrushes
- scrap paper 2" x 3" (5 x 8 cm)
- construction paper 9" x 12" (23 x 30.5 cm)

Project Notes

- Wash meat trays with soap and water to help the paint adhere better.
- Let children use their name chops to sign child-authored books, paintings, creative writing projects, etc.
- This process may also be used to make prints of animals, plants, etc.

Let's Talk About It

How is printing different in different cultures?

Why was the printing process an important development in history?

What everyday items are the product of a printing process?

ArtWorks for Kids • EMC 761

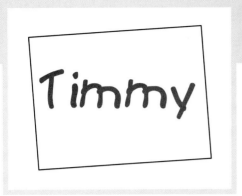

step 1

step 2

step 3

step 4

Steps to Follow

1 Give each child a piece of foam block, a small piece of scrap paper, and a pencil. Ask them to print their names clearly and firmly on the paper.

2 Place the scrap paper facedown on the block. If the name has been written firmly enough, it will be visible through the paper. Now trace over these letters to press them into the block. The letters are now written on the block backwards.

3 **Lightly** paint the surface of the block with tempera paint. Experiment to discover what level of paint coverage is the most effective.

4 Gently press the name chop onto a piece of scrap paper as a test. Lift the name chop to see the print. The name should be clearly shown.

5 Apply a new coat of paint. Print on the construction paper a number of times to create a pattern. Wipe off the name chop between prints.

Rubber Stamp

Create a rubber stamp to use on stationery, cards, gift tags, bookmarks, or as a signature stamp.

Vocabulary

medium   positive space

negative space   printing

Materials

- scrap paper
- pencil
- Safety Kut® Printing Medium—2" x 3" (5 x 8 cm) block per child or large rubber erasers
- broad-tipped watercolor markers
- carving tools
- stencils or small cookie cutters
- construction paper

Project Notes

- When demonstrating with the carving tool, always point out safety rules:

  Keep free hand back from cutter and close to body.

  Carve away from body.

  Carve away only small bits at a time.

- Use watercolor markers so color may be removed easily with water. Clean off the printing medium with a damp towel before changing color.

- Keep the design simple. Do not use letters.

- Work quickly when printing so the marker doesn't dry.

Let's Talk About It

What is the proper way to handle carving tools?

Talk about positive and negative space.

ArtWorks for Kids • EMC 761

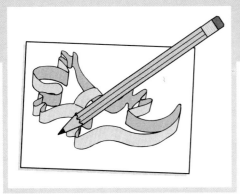

step 1

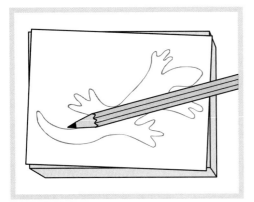

step 2

step 3

Steps to Follow

1 Make a design on scrap paper by tracing around a stencil or small cookie cutter. Retrace the image firmly so it can be seen through the back of the sheet of paper.

2 Turn the scrap paper over onto the print block material. Retrace the image to create an outline on the block. Determine which is the positive part of the design and which is the negative or surrounding space.

3 Use a carving tool to carve out the design. Decide whether to carve out the positive or the negative area of the design.

4 Spread watercolor marker on the printing surface of the block. Turn the block over quickly and print on the scrap paper.

5 When children are comfortable with printing, they may print on the final paper. Let children experiment with various ways to fill a sheet of paper by using the same design over and over again. How can various color combinations affect the final result?

Positive or negative?

The same design might be carved on both sides of the block. One side will have the positive (the background) cut out and the other side will have the negative (the figure or design) cut out. Line up the block with the edge of the paper and print one design beside the other by flipping the block over and lining it up.

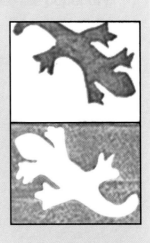

ArtWorks for Kids • EMC 761

What Is Printing ?

Printing is an art form where an image is transferred by means of ink or paint to another surface. The printing tool itself becomes the image. The printed image may be made by the cross sections of an apple or a green pepper, by something as simple as a piece of string, or by a carved design on a block of wood. The nice thing about printing tools is that they can be used again and again!

Printing is valuable in teaching the basic principles of design. Children learn to repeat shapes and colors to build interesting patterns. Whatever the type of printing, allow children plenty of time to explore different design possibilities when creating a printed picture.

Recyclables

ArtWorks for Kids • EMC 761

Papier-Mâché Trays

Create a decorative tray using recycled newspapers and foam meat trays while learning the art of papier-mâché.

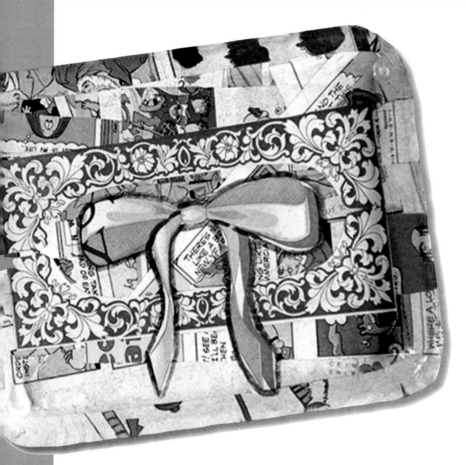

Vocabulary

papier-mâché

Materials

- foam meat trays (any color or size)
- magazines
- newspapers (torn or cut into strips)
- water
- scissors
- bowls for mixture
- papier-mâché mixture
- varnish
- white glue
- paintbrush

Let's Talk About It

What is papier-mâché? Who invented it?

What does papier-mâché mean?

Why is papier-mâché considered a form of sculpture?

Project Notes

- Wash all foam trays in soapy water and dry them before starting.
- Set up a work area and have children wear smocks.
- Have children dip each piece of paper in the papier-mâché mixture rather than place the paper strips into the mixture all at once. This keeps the paper from breaking down too much.
- The varnish should be applied in a well-ventilated area by an adult.

Steps to Follow

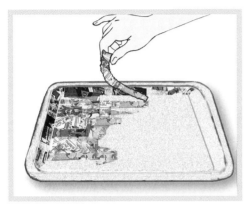

steps 1 & 2

1 Tear newspapers into strips. Make the papier-mâché mixture in bowls or buckets.

2 Dip each strip of paper in the papier-mâché mixture. Smooth the excess glue from the strip of paper before placing it on the tray. Too much glue will result in long drying times.

3 Smooth and overlap each piece of paper so that the ends are tidy. Follow the form of the tray. After one side of the tray is covered, let it dry.

step 3

4 Proceed to the other side of the tray. Overlap each piece of paper until the surface is covered. Let it dry throughly.

5 Cut colorful pictures from magazines. Dip these pictures in the papier-mâché mixture and smooth them onto the front of the tray. Let the tray dry. Then cover the back of the tray with pictures.

step 5

6 When the tray is completely dry, protect the surface by brushing on a coat of white glue.

Papier-mâché can be created from different kinds of mixtures

Method 1—Use one part glue to two parts water and mix well.

Method 2—Use wallpaper paste mixed according to package directions.

Collage Containers

Create a pot or bowl from a discarded plastic jug while learning about collage.

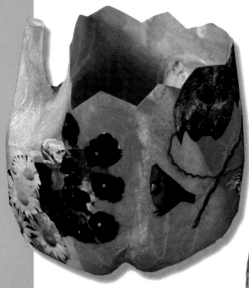

Vocabulary

collage   design

Materials

- plastic milk jugs or detergent bottles
- scissors
- glue—equal parts white glue and water
- bowls (for glue mixture)
- paintbrush
- cords or strings
- magazine pictures
- tissue or wrapping paper
- spray varnish (optional)

Project Notes

- Use small pictures from magazines to decorate the jugs. Pictures of flowers, birds, or small animals fit the theme of this project.

- Have children wear smocks and work in a designated area, as this project can be messy.

Let's Talk About It

Compare the techniques of collage and papier-mâché.

What kinds of materials might be used in making a collage?

Why is it important to overlap materials when doing collage?

ArtWorks for Kids • EMC 761

Steps to Follow

steps 2 & 3

step 1

step 5

1 Wash a discarded plastic bottle or jug and dry it. Cut off the top and make it the desired size.

2 Cut up the tissue or wrapping paper into small pieces. Brush glue on the surface of the jug. Lay the paper pieces on the glued surface and brush glue over them. Let this layer dry completely.

3 Cut pictures from discarded magazines or junk mail. Collect bits of string or cord to add to the collage.

4 Add the pictures and other items to the jug, using the glue mixture and the brush. Make sure all edges are glued securely. Develop a pleasing design by overlapping the pictures and gluing them in place. The key to good collage is overlapping the paper edges carefully.

5 When the collage is complete, set the jug aside to dry overnight. Then spray on varnish, if desired.

What is collage?

Collage is an art technique that utilizes a variety of papers and fabrics to create a design or picture. The various pieces are glued together onto a background of paper or cardboard or other objects.

Scrapbooks

Create a scrapbook using recycled cardboard and newspapers while learning a basic form of bookbinding.

Vocabulary

bookbinding

endpapers

hinge

recycled

Materials

- tagboard
- newspaper
- white glue mixed with a small amount of water
- paintbrush
- ruler
- pencil
- paper cutter or heavy-duty scissors
- a hole punch
- yarn or shoelaces

Let's Talk About It

What other materials might be used to create a covering for a book or portfolio?

Discuss the different ways the tie binding may be wrapped.

Project Notes

- A paper cutter is helpful for cutting the heavy cardboard.
- Use this scrapbook as a class journal or as a portfolio in which children collect class work they want to save and share.

steps 1 & 2

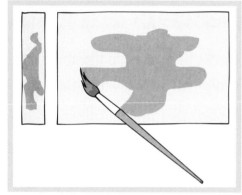

step 4

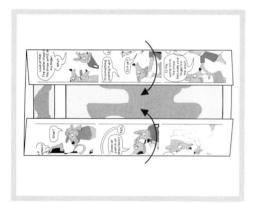

step 5

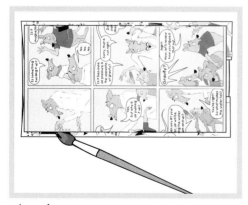

step 6

Steps to Follow

1. Cut the tagboard to the desired size using a ruler to measure. Cut off a 2" (5 cm) section of each piece of tagboard. This small section will act as a hinge when the two pieces are joined with the newspaper.

2. Choose sheets of newspaper with interesting print. The comics make a colorful cover. Cut two rectangles that are larger than the tagboard. Lay them out on a large surface.

3. Place the tagboard pieces in the center of the newspaper sheet. Draw around each piece of tagboard with a pencil.

4. Remove the tagboard. Place the tagboard on a flat surface and brush one side of it with the glue and water mixture. Place the tagboard glue-side down back on the newspaper in the area designated by the pencil outlines.

5. Brush glue around the edges of the tagboard. Fold the newspaper border over and press it into the glue.

6. Cut newspaper sheets for the endpapers (inside covering). Brush glue on the inside of the tagboard and lay the newspaper in place over it.

7. When both covers are complete and the glue is dry, punch holes in the left margins and use shoelaces or yarn to hold the book together.

ArtWorks for Kids • EMC 761

Junk Frames

Create a picture frame using cardboard and recycled materials.

Vocabulary

design

free form

three-dimensional

Materials

- 2 pieces of cardboard the same size
- white paste or glue with applicator
- found objects—straws, bottle tops, can tabs, string, etc.
- scissors
- masking tape

Project Notes

- Use leftover cardboard from writing tablets, cereal boxes, etc. Collect and share pieces of different sizes, shapes, and colors.

Let's Talk About It

How does working with three-dimensional objects add new challenges to creating a design?

What kinds of theme frames might be created to complement certain photos or works of art?

Steps to Follow

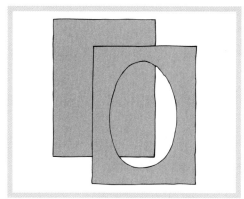

step 2

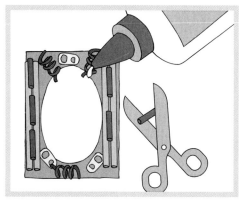

step 3

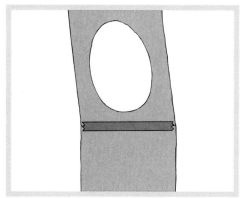

step 4

1 Each child will need two pieces of cardboard of the same size.

2 Cut a square, circle, or free-form shape from the center of one piece of cardboard to make the frame.

3 Glue the "found objects" to the frame. Glue the larger pieces first. Be aware of the design that is developing. Vary lengths, colors, and sizes of objects.

4 When the glue is dry, place the frame over the other piece of cardboard. Make sure edges are even. Flip the top piece up and connect the two frame parts with masking tape (on the inside) to form a hinge.

5 Insert a favorite piece of artwork or a photo and tape it in place.

Design principles to consider

• Repetition of shapes, lines, or colors

Repeating shapes in a design can lend continuity.

• Variation of sizes and shapes

Using large and small objects adds interest to a design.

• Contrasting colors in a pattern

Use of contrasting colors creates a design that is easier to see.

       ArtWorks for Kids • EMC 761

Window Hangings

Practice tinsmithing techniques while making a decorative hanging.

Vocabulary

folk art

stencil

tinsmithing

Materials

- tinfoil pie plates
- nails
- a hammer or a block of wood
- thick cardboard remnants
- folk art patterns or stencils
- pencil and paper
- string

Project Notes

- Safety should be emphasized in this project because children are working with hammers and nails.

- Foil plates are best. Children will have an easier time tracing the pattern onto the plate and minimal effort is needed to punch the design with the nail. Work on pieces of cardboard to avoid marring the table or floor surface.

Let's Talk About It

How is tinsmithing different from other art forms such as carving or weaving?

What kinds of objects would a tinsmith make?

Steps to Follow

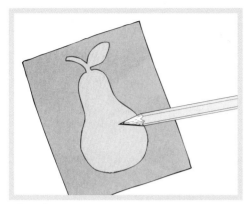

step 1

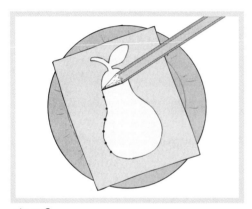

step 2

step 3

1 Trace a simple pattern onto paper to serve as a stencil.

2 Place the pattern on the inside flat surface of the pie plate. Trace the pattern with a pencil, making slight indentations in the soft foil. Remove the pattern.

3 Put the plate on a piece of thick cardboard. Using a nail and a hammer, punch holes following the pattern lines. Only a tap is needed to punch the hole. Keep the holes at least 1/4" (0.6 cm) but not more than 1/2" (1.25 cm) apart.

4 Hold the finished piece to the light to check for areas that may need extra holes.

5 Punch a hole for a string loop. Hang the project in a window and let the light stream through.

Typical folk art designs

ArtWorks for Kids • EMC 761

Zuni Fetishes

Practice simple carving techniques while learning about a Native American art form.

Vocabulary

carving

fetish

sculpture

Zuni

Materials

- bars of soap (leftovers are perfect)
- water in cups
- plastic knives or carving tools
- toothpicks
- yarn or string
- pebbles, beads, feathers

Project Notes

- Have children bring in leftover bars of soap. Soften the soap remnants by soaking in water and then form into pieces big enough to carve.

- Look at books and pictures of fetishes made by the Zuni tribe. Discuss this art form and its uses. Be sure children are respectful of this aspect of Zuni life.

- Young children might use plastic knives to carve, while older children can use carving tools. Discuss safety rules before carving.

Let's Talk About It

How is carving different from sculpting? How are they the same?

Why is carving considered an art form?

What kinds of materials and tools do carvers use?

Many ancient groups of people carved ceremonial pieces and tools. How do modern people use carvings today?

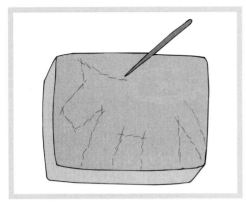

step 1

step 2

step 5

Steps to Follow

1 Look at pictures of fetishes or simple animal shapes. Use a toothpick to draw a simple outline shape on the soap piece.

2 Carve away small pieces of soap at a time. If the soap cracks, wet it with water and smooth with a finger. Whittle away each area slowly until you have carved out the basic shape you want.

3 Once the animal is carved, smooth the edges with water. Children may use a toothpick to add details such as eyes, feathers, or fur.

4 Let the fetish dry on a paper towel. Reposition the carving occasionally so it doesn't stick to the paper.

5 Once the carving is completely dry, use pieces of yarn or string to tie pebbles, beads, or feathers around the fetish in Zuni fashion.

3-D Paper Decorations

Use paper-folding techniques to create a three-dimensional decoration from old magazines.

Vocabulary

decoration

three-dimensional

Materials

- magazines (all sizes)
- spray paints (all colors)
- string
- stapler

Project Notes

- Create different patterns by changing the folds:

    fold pages twice instead of once

    fold half the pages, then flip the magazine around and continue folding to create an interesting twisted pattern

    Let children experiment with different folds to discover the effects they can create.

- A light layer of gold or silver spray paint gives a gilded look.

Let's Talk About It

How was dimension created in this project?

In what ways can this be used besides as a decoration?

What is the art of Japanese paper folding called? (origami)

step 1

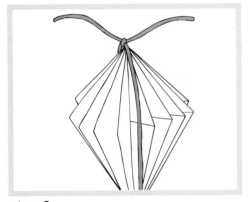

step 2

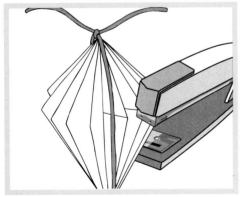

step 3

Steps to Follow

1 Give each child a magazine. Start by folding each page from the top right corner to the center spine of the magazine. Then fold the bottom corner into the spine. Crease folds firmly. Continue in this manner until all pages are folded.

2 Once the pages are folded, loop the string through the center of the magazine and tie it, leaving enough string to hang the decoration.

3 Bend the front cover around to meet the back cover, creating a three-dimensional shape. Staple the covers together. (If the magazine is very thin, fold two magazines and staple them together.)

4 Spray the decoration with several colors of paint. An adult should do the spraying in a well-ventilated area.

5 Hang the decoration to dry.

Designer Soap Boxes

Learn about camouflage while creating a storage container from reusable detergent boxes.

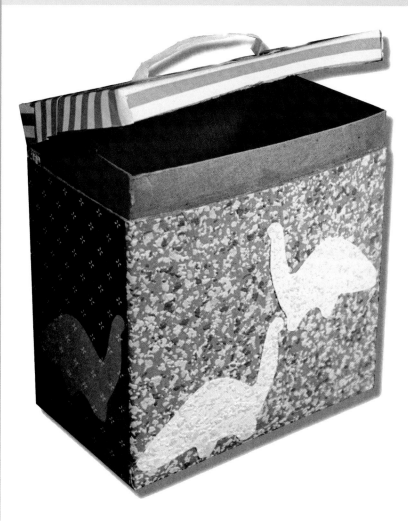

Vocabulary

camouflage

optical illusion

Materials

- empty laundry detergent boxes with lids
- wallpaper remnants (contrasting colors)
- cookie cutters or stencils
- pencil
- scissors
- glue, diluted with water
- paintbrush
- newspapers

Project Notes

- Plan ahead and ask local wallpaper stores to save out-of-date sample books for you. Most paper patterns in the books will have the same pattern repeated in different color choices. These are perfect for this project.

Let's Talk About It

How is camouflage used in nature?

How is camouflage used by humans?

Can you think of ways camouflage has been used in art?

ArtWorks for Kids • EMC 761

Steps to Follow

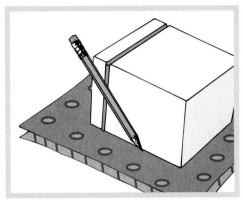

step 2

step 3

step 4

1 Choose wallpaper remnants with the same or a similar pattern, but in different colors. Plan which paper will go on each side of the box and lid.

2 Lay the box on the wallpaper pieces and trace around the edges with a pencil. Cut out the pieces.

3 Lay the cut pieces of wallpaper facedown on sheets of newspaper. Brush on the glue. Place the glued paper on the box. Cover the entire surface.

4 Use a pencil to trace around the cookie cutters or stencils on the extra pieces of wallpaper. Cut out the images and glue them to the box. If using striped papers, try to match them in a way that "hides" the shape most effectively.

5 Allow the box to dry and use the "designer" box for storage.

The designs in this project are built with images laid on top of a figured background. The goal is to create these shapes from another figured paper that blends subtly into the background design.

ArtWorks for Kids • EMC 761

Luminaries

Use various tools to make a luminary from reusable cans.

Vocabulary

design   tinsmithing

luminary

Materials

- metal cans (all shapes and sizes)
- rotary can opener
- punch can opener
- hammer
- nails
- spray paint (all colors)
- newspaper
- votive candle and tinfoil pad
- pencil
- stencils (optional)

Project Notes

- Safety should be emphasized in this project. Thick gloves are advised. It might be best to have an adult wash the cans, punch the holes, and flatten the sharp points for younger children.

- Have children collect cans and wash them carefully to remove any residue. Remove bottoms with a rotary can opener.

- Encourage children to work all the way around the can so light shines through evenly.

- Provide plenty of room for working with the hammer. You may want to set up a safety zone for this activity.

Let's Talk About It

How was the art of tinsmithing used in this project?

What other materials could be used to make luminaries?

Luminaries have been used in many cultures. What uses do you know about?

Steps to Follow

1 Use a pencil to lightly outline the design to be created on the can. Or invent the design as you work.

2 Begin working with the can openers. Use the punch can opener around the top and bottom edges of the can to make triangular holes. Flatten any sharp points. Use a hammer and nail to punch holes around the side of the can. Tap lightly to avoid collapsing the can.

3 When the design is finished, decorate the can using spray paint. Stencils may be used to add to the design. Cover the paint area generously with newspaper. Always spray paint in an outside area away from heat and with plenty of ventilation.

4 Place the luminary over a lit votive candle that is sitting on a tinfoil pad. Watch the light patterns shine through the holes.

step 1

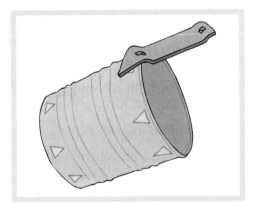

step 2

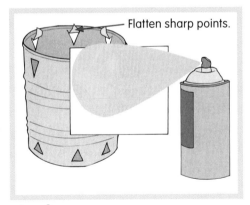

step 3

How to use a stencil

1. Cut the shape from a sturdy paper. (Or use a precut commercial stencil.)

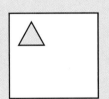

2. Hold the form on the area to be painted. Spray paint lightly over the stencil.

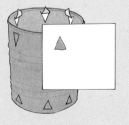

ArtWorks for Kids • EMC 761

Crayon Candles

Learn candle making while using reusable products.

Vocabulary

candlewick   mold   paraffin

Materials

- broken crayons (without paper coverings)
- wax (paraffin)
- wicking or string
- candy thermometer
- double boiler
- molds (milk cartons, yogurt cups, cans, etc.)
- color wheel (see page 28)
- vegetable oil
- heat source
- newspapers

Let's Talk About It

Discuss how and why candles were first used.

Look at different types of candles. How are they alike and different?

Some candles are made of beeswax. What texture do these candles have?

Project Notes

- Always use caution when working with hot wax. Never melt wax directly on a heat source—always use a double boiler. The boiling water will keep the wax from burning. **All** melting and pouring of hot wax should be done by an adult.
- Work over newspapers for easy cleanup.
- Two-color layered candles can be made by pouring one color, letting it set, and then pouring the other color.

Steps to Follow

steps 2 & 3

step 4

step 6

1. Look at a color wheel to sort crayons into "mixable" color piles. To make a green candle, add green crayons to the wax or mix blue and yellow crayons in the wax to make green.

2. Make sure the molds are clean. Lightly coat the inside with cooking oil for easier unmolding of the finished candle.

3. Poke a tiny hole in the bottom of the mold for adding the wick. Thread a wick or string through the hole and tie a knot on the outside of the mold (or use metal wick bases found in craft stores—these clamp onto the wick and sit in the base of the mold).

4. To guarantee a straight wick in the candle, tie the top of the wick to a pencil. Set the pencil across the top of the mold.

5. Break the paraffin into pieces and put in the top of a double boiler along with a thermometer. Heat the wax. When the wax reaches approximately 175° Fahrenheit (80° Celsius), add the crayons. Use the equivalent of three crayons per cup of wax.

6. When crayons are melted, carefully pour the mixture into the molds.

7. Let the candle set for at least three hours before unmolding. Paper molds such as milk cartons can be simply torn away.

Paper Bag Portraits

Create a mosaic portrait using torn colored-paper bags.

Vocabulary

mosaic

portrait

Materials

- lightweight cardboard (any size)
- white glue mixed with a small amount of water
- paintbrushes for glue
- colorful paper bags
- cups
- pencils

Project Notes

- For this project collect paper bags with different colors printed on them: pet food bags, grocery bags, old gift bags, etc.
- Show portraits done by famous artists and compare their styles.
- Talk about placement of facial features to help children plan their portraits.

Let's Talk About It

How is a mosaic different from a painted portrait?

What other materials could be used to create a portrait?

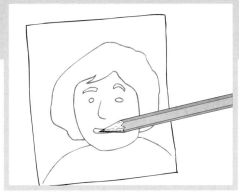

step 1

step 2

step 3

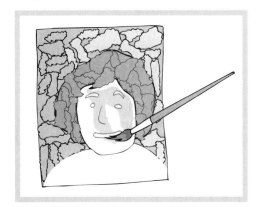

step 4

Steps to Follow

1 Draw a simple portrait of a friend. Sketch it in pencil on the cardboard. Use an oval for the face and add the eyebrows, eyes, nose, and mouth. Keep it simple.

2 Tear the bags into small pieces. Sort the pieces into piles by color. Children can plan what colors and textures they will use in their mosaic.

3 Brush glue on the background area. Then place the colored bag pieces on the glue. Continue until the background is completely covered by using the brush to help smooth pieces down. Keep fingers clean. The glue will dry clear. It is a good idea to overlap pieces.

4 Apply the glue to the hair and then add the torn paper.

5 Now begin on the face. Place the pieces of torn paper to follow the contours of the face. After the "skin" is covered, fill in the lips, eyes, and eyebrows. Tear the colored pieces to fit the small areas such as eyes and lips.

6 Add clothing, a hat, or other details.

7 Make sure all the paper pieces are glued securely. Set the mosaic aside to dry.

Paper Quilts

Create a quilt design using wallpaper remnants.

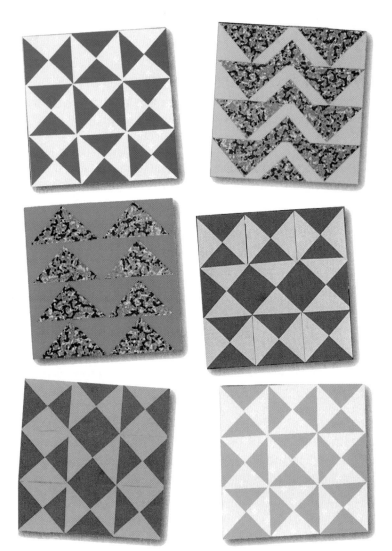

Vocabulary

contrast

design

patterning

repetition

symmetrical

Materials

- wallpaper remnants
- scissors
- glue stick
- construction paper or colored mat board cut in a 6" (15 cm) square
- ruler
- pencil

Project Notes

- Weaving is mainly repetition and patterning. It involves organization of color and texture into a pleasing design. Although quilting is not thought of as weaving, the repetition of color and design is valuable when learning to pattern. It helps to talk first about patterning and the repetition of color and shape when working on this project. Show quilt patterns to children, then show a weaving such as a rug that has a definite pattern.

Let's Talk About It

Can you see how a weaver uses color, shape, and repetition to create the desired pattern in a weaving?

Why is it easier to design with paper first instead of designing directly on the loom?

ArtWorks for Kids • EMC 761

Steps to Follow

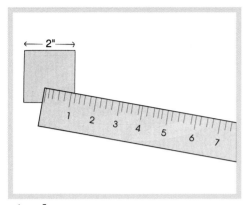
step 1

1 Choose a wallpaper remnant for color and contrast. Using a ruler and pencil, measure and cut the remnant into 2" (5 cm) squares.

2 Cut the squares diagonally to form triangles and then cut those diagonally again.

step 2

3 Place the triangles on the colored paper or board and arrange in a pleasing design. Be aware of repeating shapes when planning.

4 Glue the triangles in place.

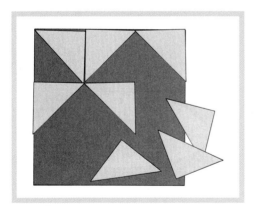
step 3

Typical quilt patterns

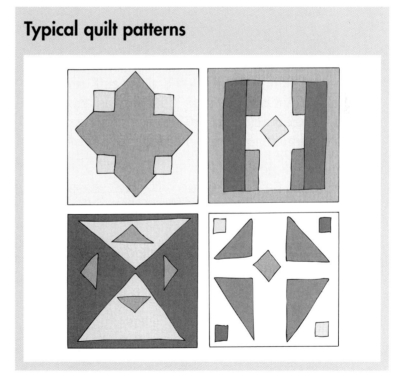

ArtWorks for Kids • EMC 761

Japanese Dolls

Create a Japanese doll from reusable paper items while learning paper-folding techniques.

Vocabulary

kimono   obi   origami

Materials

- paper towel tube
- white glue or hot glue
- head—white tissue paper
  6" x 3" (15 x 8 cm)
- hair—blue tissue paper
  6" x 2" (15 x 5 cm)
- wrapping paper (assorted colors)
  first neckband—2" x 6" (5 x 15 cm)
  second neckband—4" x 8" (10 x 20 cm)
  underdress—6" x 7" (15 x 18 cm)
  outer kimono—10" x 7" (25.5 x 18 cm)
  obi—2" x 6" (5 x 15 cm)
- cotton balls
- craft stick
- stapler
- 2 ball-top straight pins (optional)
- fine-point felt pens—red and black

Project Notes

- Have children collect paper tubes and used wrapping paper ahead of time.
- If papers are wrinkled, you may iron them on a low setting or press them between books.

Let's Talk About It

Why is paper folding important in this project?

Why is it important to follow each step when creating a craft project?

How is the texture of the face and hair different from the kimono?

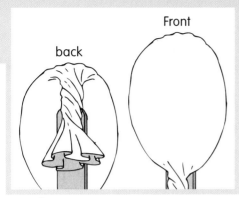

back   Front

step 1

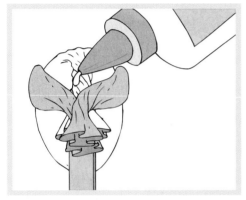

step 2

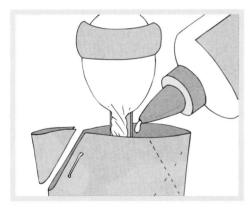

step 3

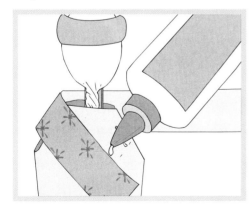

step 4

Steps to Follow

1 Make the head.
Lay the white tissue on a clean surface and place one or two cotton balls in the center. Fold the paper lengthwise over the cotton balls and twist the ends together tightly.

Glue the head to one end of the craft stick, keeping the twisted ends facing down.

Draw eyes and a mouth with felt pens.

2 Make the hair.
Place one cotton ball in the center of the tissue. Pull the cotton ball a little for a slightly longer shape, then roll it in the tissue. Wrap the roll around the top of the head.

Twist the ends in the back and glue in place.

3 Place the craft stick with the head attached into the top of the paper tube and glue in place.

Staple the top of the tube closed on either side of the stick. Snip the corners of the tube at an angle for shoulders.

4 Make the neckbands.
Fold the first neckband in half the long way. Lay the neck of the tube on the center of this paper. Fold the paper to the front like a scarf and glue in place.

Repeat this process with the second neckband, laying it slightly below the first neckband. (See picture on next page, step 5.)

Japanese Dolls

step 5

step 6

5 Make the underdress. Wrap the bottom half of the tube with the underdress paper. Glue in place.

6 Make the outer kimono. Fold down 1 1/4" (3 cm) along the long edge of the outer kimono paper. Place the neck portion of the tube on the top center of the kimono and fold over like a scarf. Glue in place.

Take the outer corners of the paper kimono and fold to the center to make sleeves. Glue in place. The arms will look folded.

7 Make the obi (sash). Fold the wrapping paper in fourths the long way. Wrap it around the hip area, securing with glue. Add a bow if you wish.

8 You may add a fan to the back of the head. Accordion-fold some paper and glue the ends together. Then glue the fan to the back of the head. Add two ball-top pins in the hair for decoration.

Making dolls has been a serious art form in Japan since the seventeenth century. Many dolls are made of plaster, rice paper, or silk.

 ArtWorks for Kids • EMC 761

Nature

Handmade Paper

Create handmade papers containing dried flowers and leaves while learning the art of papermaking.

Vocabulary

deckle paper

mold fiber

Materials

- recyclable paper scraps
- small flowers and leaves (dried and pressed)
- scissors
- a mold and deckle (see directions on page 133)
- absorbent fabric (such as felt or a blanket)
- large dishpan or sink
- blender
- water
- sponge

Let's Talk About It

How is the texture of handmade paper different from machine-made paper?

What kinds of natural fibers can be used in making paper?

Project Notes

- Some papers will be thin and some will be thick depending on the type of recyclable paper being used.
- You may trim the paper sheets to create straight edges or leave them as they come off the mold with ragged edges.

step 2

step 3

step 4

step 6

Steps to Follow

1 Cut and tear small pieces of recyclable paper and soak in water to soften.

2 Place approximately 1/4 cup (60 ml) of paper in the blender and fill with water. (You may also add small leaves and flower bits as long as the paper content exceeds the amount of plant matter.)

3 Fill the sink or dishpan with water. Pour the blended mixture into the water until you have a thin layer of fiber floating on the top of the water. Add the pressed leaves and flowers to this mixture. You may even add glitter to liven up the texture.

4 Place the mold on top of the deckle screen. Hold them firmly together. Dip into the dishpan and scoop up a layer of the mixture onto the screen.

5 Transfer the sheet of fiber to a damp piece of absorbent fabric by removing the mold and placing the deckle, on the fabric with the paper side down.

6 Press repeatedly on the back of the deckle with a sponge to release the paper. Gently lift the deckle, leaving the paper on the fabric. Let the paper dry 3 to 24 hours.

How to make a mold and deckle

Materials
- 2 small frames the same size

- screening with small holes

- thumbtacks

mold

(a frame)

deckle

(a frame, the same size as the mold, with fiberglass, plastic, or wire screen)

Gourd Rattles

Create a gourd rattle using Native American designs.

Vocabulary

design

earth tones

gourd

pictograph

Materials

- dried gourds
- tempera paints (various colors)
- paintbrushes (small)
- pencils
- samples of Native American designs
- spray varnish (optional)

Project Notes

- Dried gourds may be found in the autumn at many markets. Choose gourds that can easily be handled by the children.

- Study Native American designs before working on this project. Be sensitive to the meaning of the designs you choose to use. Some Native American designs are strictly ornamental, but others may have spiritual meanings and should not be used.

- The painted gourds may be hung or set on cups to dry.

Let's Talk About It

What are some ways in which gourds can be used?

Why do Native Americans paint the gourds?

How do pictographs tell stories?

Why are earth tones used in this project?

What are earth tones?

Earth tones are the paint hues that resemble the muted colors found in nature: brown, gray-green, rust, beige, etc.

ArtWorks for Kids • EMC 761

Steps to Follow

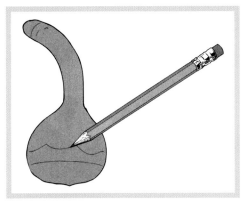

step 2

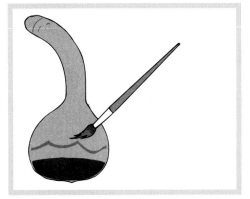

step 3

1 Remove any dirt or residue from the gourds before painting begins.

2 Trace simple designs onto the gourd with a pencil. The designs may be ornamental or they may tell a story. Plan the color scheme. Native Americans use earth tones to decorate their gourds.

3 Paint the gourds starting with the light colors first. Let the paint dry completely between color changes.

4 You may want to spray the gourd with a clear finish when it is completed. This will protect the paint. Be sure to do this in a well-ventilated area.

Sample pictographs

Pine Needle Dolls

Create a doll using pine needles.

Vocabulary

folk art

pine needles

Materials

- pine needles (long)
- string
- scissors

Project Notes

- Collect a lot of pine needles, dried or fresh, so each child can have a large handful.

- Young children will need to work with a partner. One child can hold the needles while the other ties the string. Children should know how to tie a simple knot before attempting to make these dolls.

Let's Talk About It

What other resources from nature could be used to make dolls?

In what cultures can you find dolls made from natural materials?

ArtWorks for Kids • EMC 761

Steps to Follow

1 Make two groups of needles, a large group for the body and a smaller one for the arms.

2 Make the arms.
Lay the needles for the arms on the table.

Cut two pieces of string long enough to wrap around the arm twice and have enough left over to tie a knot. Lay each string approximately 1/2" (1.25 cm) from each end. Tie the strings tightly and make a knot on each end. Trim the needles so the ends are even.

3 Make the body.
Place the needles for the body on the table.

Wrap a piece of string around the pine needles approximately 1/2" (1.25 cm) down from the top. Tie with a knot. This creates the "hair."

Tie a second piece of string 1" (2.5 cm) from the previous string. This creates the "head."

4 Separate the needles into two groups. Slip the arm group between the needles.

Tie a piece of string around the pine needles below the arms to form the waist of the doll. This will also hold the arms in place.

The remaining needles form the impression of a skirt. If you prefer legs instead of a skirt, separate the needles into two groups and tie off each end to form feet.

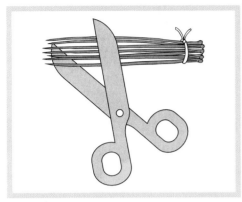
step 2

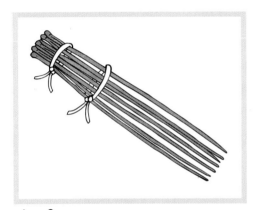
step 3

step 4

 ArtWorks for Kids • EMC 761

Raffia Mats

Use basic weaving skills to create a small mat from natural raffia.

Vocabulary

raffia

warp

weft

Materials

- raffia
- cardboard
- scissors
- pencil and straight edge
- tape
- glue
- a plate (5" [13 cm] diameter)

Project Notes

- Raffia can be found at most art supply stores and in school supply catalogs. Raffia does not have to be cut. It can be used in the random lengths in which it comes.

Let's Talk About It

What kinds of natural materials are used in weavings?

What other useful objects could be woven from raffia?

How is the texture of raffia different from other weaving materials?

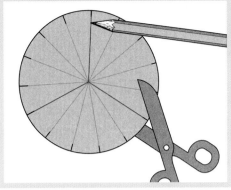

step 1

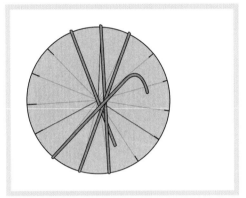

step 2

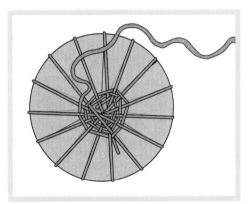

step 3

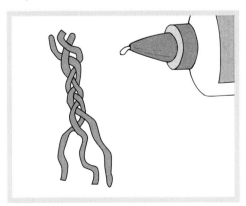

step 5

Steps to Follow

1 Make the cardboard weaving frame by tracing around a plate.

Using a pencil, divide the frame into thirds. Then divide each third into 5 parts. Now there will be 15 sections. An adult will need to do this for younger children.

Make a small notch at the edge of each line to hold the warp strands.

2 Create the warp.
Fasten one end of a raffia strand to the frame with tape. Begin creating the warp by winding the raffia from each notch to the opposite notch, working around the frame until all notches have been used. The end of the raffia strand may be taped to keep it in place.

3 Begin weaving the weft.
Using a separate strand of raffia, begin weaving in and out of the warp strands. Work from the center toward the outer edge. Keep the weft close so the weaving will not have holes or gaps.

When the weaving is finished, tie off the weft strand to make it secure.

4 Weave the other side of the frame in the same manner.

5 Make a decorative border around the mat by braiding a piece of raffia and securing it to the edge with glue. (See page 44.)

Raffia Plates

Practice basic weaving skills by creating a Native American-style plate using natural raffia.

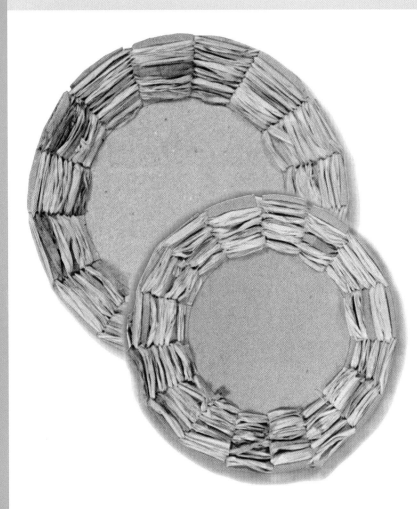

Vocabulary

raffia

warp

weft

Materials

- cardboard
- round plates or bowls, one about 2" (5 cm) larger in diameter than the other
- scissors
- raffia
- white glue
- pencil

Project Notes

- The act of weaving in and out of the cardboard tabs teaches the rhythm and pattern of weaving. It also teaches the importance of keeping the weaving material tight and uniform. These are invaluable skills when learning to braid or weave a more intricate piece. Any size cardboard disk may be used.
- Have an adult make the cardboard weaving frame for younger children.

Let's Talk About It

How is weaving used to manufacture clothing, blankets, or carpets?

Which part of the bowl is the warp?

What natural products other than raffia are used in making baskets?

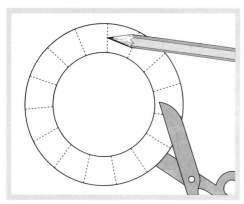
step 1

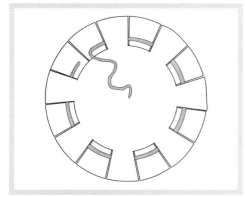
step 2a

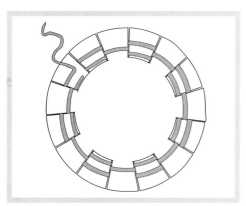
step 2b

Steps to Follow

1 Make a weaving frame.
Using the larger plate or bowl, trace a circle onto a piece of cardboard.

Trace the smaller plate or bowl inside the larger circle.

Using the pencil, divide the outer circle into 15 parts.

Cut on the lines from the outside edge to the inner circle line only. This will give you the base of the plate and the tabs (warp) to weave around.

2 Weave the bowl.
Start weaving with a piece of raffia going in and out of the warp tabs. The raffia will be the weft.

Add on pieces of raffia as you go. No tying is needed, but some children may want to glue the end of the raffia piece to the cardboard before starting with a new piece. Make sure not to skip a tab as you weave in and out.

After you weave a few strands of raffia, push each row next to the previous row with your fingers to create a tight weave. Repeat this process often as you weave the bowl.

After all the weaving is finished, glue the end of the last raffia strand to the cardboard or tuck it behind the woven pieces.

         ArtWorks for Kids • EMC 761

Sand Candles

Create a free form candle using wax and sand.

Vocabulary

free form

paraffin

wick

Materials

- sand
- wax (paraffin)
- wicking or string
- candy thermometer
- double boiler
- deep pan or tub
- heat source
- water
- broken crayons (paper removed)
- toothpicks

Let's Talk About It

Why are these candles considered free form?

What natural resources were used in making this candle?

How is the texture of the sand different from the texture of the wax?

Why was sand necessary to create this candle?

Project Notes

- Always use caution when working with hot wax. Never melt wax directly on a heat source; always use a double boiler. An adult must pour the wax.

- Old crayons are used to add color to the wax.

Steps to Follow

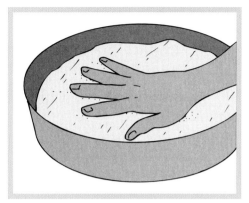

step 2

step 3

step 4

1 Begin by putting sand into a tub or deep pan. Add enough water to make the sand damp (not wet).

2 Break pieces of wax into the melting pot. Add the thermometer and heat the wax to 175° Fahrenheit (80° Celsius).

3 While the wax is melting, create a mold in the sand. Have younger children press one of their hands into the sand to make an impression at least 1/2" (1.25 cm) deep. Older children may want to create an interesting shape or irregular design in the sand.

Place a toothpick standing straight up in the center of each sand mold. This will be used later to place the wick.

4 When the wax has melted, add broken pieces of crayon. This will add color to the candle. When the crayons have melted, pour the wax into the forms pressed in the sand. **(This must be done by an adult.)** Let the wax set until it is hard (approximately one hour).

5 Dig gently under the candle and lift it out of the sand. Leave as much sand stuck to the wax as possible.

6 Remove the toothpick and insert a wick. Tie a knot in the end of the wick on the underside of the candle or secure it with a metal stopper.

Shell Flowers

Create flowers using shells from nature and basic art materials.

Vocabulary

form

shape

texture

Materials

- shells
- wire coat hangers
- wire cutters
- green tissue paper cut in 3"-wide (8 cm) strips
- green construction paper
- scissors
- glue gun and hot glue
- white glue

Project Notes

- Establish safety rules for use of the glue gun. With younger children, an adult should do this step.
- These flowers make wonderful Mother's Day gifts.

Let's Talk About It

What kinds of textures do you see and feel with your shell flower?

How does the form and shape of the shell resemble a flower?

What other natural objects could be used to make flowers?

Steps to Follow

1 Collect shells of various shapes. Wash them. If there is no access to a beach where shells can be collected, purchase them from a craft store. Talk about the different shapes and forms and what flowers they resemble.

step 2

2 Cut the wire hangers to make the stems. Start the flower by hot-gluing a length of wire to the base of the shell. Let the glue dry thoroughly.

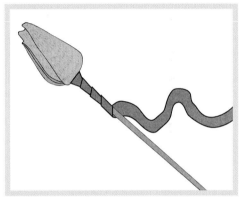

step 3

3 Take a strip of green tissue paper. Place a small amount of white glue at the base of the shell flower to hold the tissue in place. Wrap the tissue tightly around the wire. Overlap a bit as you continue down the length of the stem. Dot some white glue on the wire stem while wrapping to hold the tissue in place.

4 Cut leaves from green construction paper or the green tissue. Glue the leaves to the finished stem.

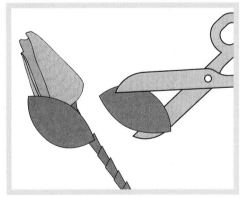

step 4

5 If you have enough materials, let children make several flowers, and arrange them in a bouquet.

Acorn Mice

Create a charming acorn mouse while learning crafting skills.

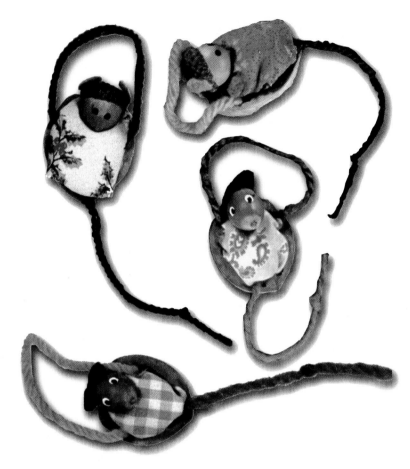

Let's Talk About It

Why is crafting important?

Do you see how some things from nature can be made to resemble other things from nature?

How are the color and texture of the acorns and walnuts alike? How are they different?

Vocabulary

acorn

craft

Materials

- acorns—heads
- walnut half shells—beds
- white glue
- 2" (5 cm) fabric squares—blankets
- cotton balls—bodies
- yarn—4" (10 cm) piece for tails
        6" (15 cm) piece for hangers
- gray or brown felt—ears
- black felt-tip marker

Project Notes

- Explain how important it is to follow directions when doing crafts projects.
- Talk about how things from nature can be formed into art. If you live in an area where it is possible, take a nature walk to collect the nuts.

steps 2 & 3

step 4

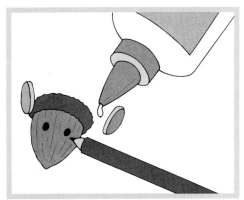

steps 5 & 6

step 7

Steps to Follow

1 Collect acorns that still have their caps. The cap looks like a hat for the mouse. If the cap has fallen off, glue it back on with white glue.

2 Fold the longer piece of yarn in half and glue it to the inside of the round sides of the walnut shell. This will be the loop for hanging the mouse.

3 Glue the smaller piece of yarn to the inside of the pointed end of the walnut shell. This will be the tail.

4 Cover a cotton ball (or two) with fabric and glue it/them to the inside of the walnut shell. Make sure all the cotton is covered and the fabric ends are glued down. This is the body of the mouse wrapped in a blanket.

5 Use a felt-tip pen to draw eyes on the mouse's face.

6 Glue pieces of felt to the head for ears.

7 Glue the head to the covered cotton at the end of the shell opposite the tail.

 ArtWorks for Kids • EMC 761

Sun Catchers

Create a sun catcher using dried flowers and wax.

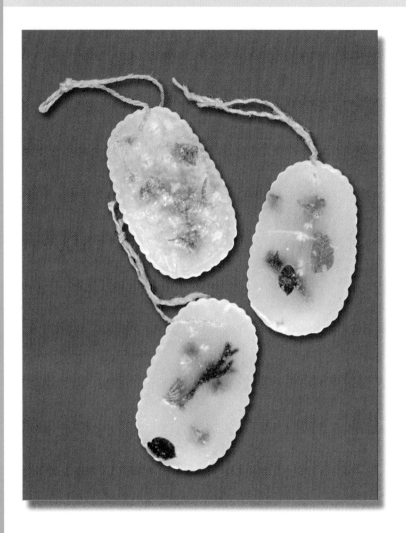

Vocabulary

color

hue

paraffin

transparent

Materials

- paraffin (wax)
- double boiler
- string
- dried flowers
- molds (such as small tart pans)
- toothpicks
- spray cooking oil

Project Notes

- Use caution when melting wax. Never melt wax directly over the heat source; always use a double boiler. **An adult must pour the wax.**

- If you do not have molds, you can use any small, shallow can.

Let's Talk About It

What colors are best for this project?

How does the transparency of the wax help this project work?

What will happen if something made with wax gets too hot?

ArtWorks for Kids • EMC 761

step 3

step 4

step 5

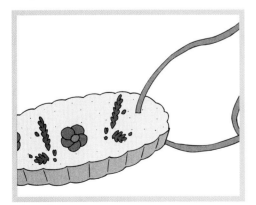

step 6

Steps to Follow

1 Collect small flowers and leaves. Set them aside to dry for several days.

2 Spray the molds with cooking oil to prevent the wax from sticking to them.

3 Melt the wax in a double boiler. When the wax has melted, pour it into the molds to a thickness of about 1/4" (0.6 cm).

4 Drop dried flowers and leaves into the wax in the mold.

5 When the wax starts to harden, place a toothpick 1/4" (0.6 cm) from the top to make a hole for the string.

6 After the wax is completely solid, remove the shape from the mold. Remove the toothpick. Thread a string through the hole. Hang the sun catcher in a shaded window. (Direct sunlight will melt the wax.)

Dried Flower Cards

Create beautiful stationery from dried and pressed flowers.

Vocabulary

arrangement

color

design

Materials

- dried flowers and leaves
- art paper—6" x 9" (15 x 23 cm)
- white glue
- books for pressing
- spray fixative (optional)

Project Notes

- Collect flowers when they are in season and press them for this project. Children enjoy seeing how different flowers look after they are pressed.
- Talk about design principles when planning these cards:

  repetition of shapes

  variation of sizes

  contrasting colors

Let's Talk About It

What textures and colors can you find in nature?

How were the dried/pressed flowers different from fresh-picked flowers?

How is arranging colors and textures important in this project?

 ArtWorks for Kids • EMC 761

Steps to Follow

step 1

step 4

1 Press fresh flowers and leaves. Put them between blotter papers or paper towels. Place them in a book or between heavy weights. Check periodically to make sure the moisture is being absorbed.

2 Fold the art paper in half to create a card.

3 Choose pressed and dried flowers, leaves, or seeds. Think about color and texture as the design is arranged.

4 Start gluing the leaves or darker colored flowers to the paper with white glue. Proceed by building up layers of flowers and leaves into a pleasing arrangement.

5 Let the card sit until all the glue is dry.

6 You may spray the card gently with a light fixative. An adult should do this in a well-ventilated area.

Making Yarn

Learn to make yarn from wool and use it in various projects such as weaving, collage, or three-dimensional sculpture.

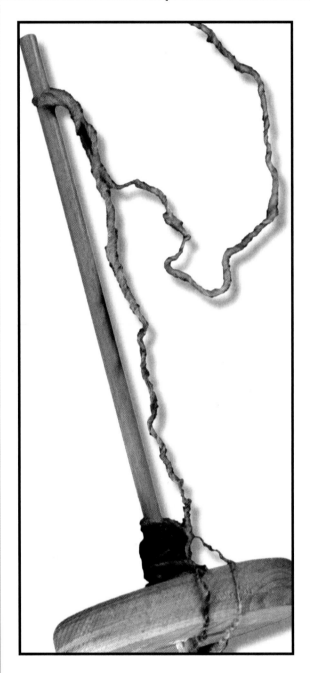

Vocabulary

carders

fiber

spin

spindle

texture

Materials

- raw wool (see notes below)
- bucket of water
- liquid soap
- carders (see notes below)
- drop spindle (see page 153)
- 18" (46 cm) strip of yarn

Project Notes

- If you are unable to find raw wool through a yarn retailer, your county agriculture cooperative may be able to help.
- Carders bought through art supply dealers are the most effective, but combs and dog brushes could be substituted. When using the combs or brushes, put the clean wool on a table and comb through it until it is straight.
- Washing the wool can be messy. Do this in a separate area that can be easily cleaned up.

Let's Talk About It

How is yarn used in creating art?

Where would natural yarn be used?

What other kinds of fibers could be used to make yarn or thread?

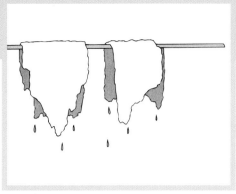

step 1

step 3

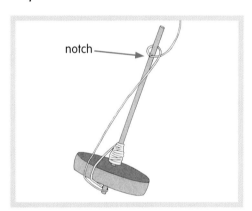

notch

step 4

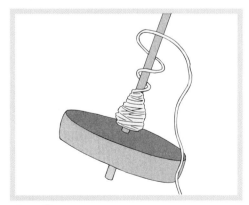

step 5

Steps to Follow

1 Collect the wool and wash small batches in a bucket of soapy water. Hang the cleaned wool to dry in a well-ventilated area.

2 Tease the wool by taking small handfuls and separating clumps and removing any dirt or debris.

3 Card the wool. Place the wool on one carder and comb the fibers with the other carder in a brushing fashion. This will make the fibers straight and ready for spinning.

4 Thread the spindle as described below. Hold the wool and yarn together and twist the spindle clockwise by the rod with the weight side down. As the yarn starts to twist, it will catch the wool and spin it to make yarn.

5 As the yarn gets longer, wrap it around the rod and restart the spinning process. This may take some practice.

How to make a drop spindle

Materials
• sanded wood circle 4" (10 cm) in diameter and 3/4" (2 cm) thick
• dowel rod 1/4" (0.6 cm) in diameter and 11" (28 cm) long

Steps to follow
1. Drill a hole directly in the center of the wood circle. Fit the dowel rod snugly into the hole. Pound the dowel through the hole until 3/4" (2 cm) of the rod sticks out on the bottom side.
2. Cut a slanted notch on the rod approximately 1" (2.5 cm) from the top.

How to thread the spindle
1. Tie the yarn strip to the rod where it meets the circle.
2. Wrap the yarn around the bottom 3/4" (2 cm) section of the rod one time.
3. Pull the yarn to the top of the rod, wrap it once, and slide it into the notch.
4. Hold the wool and yarn end in one hand. Let the spindle hang. Spin the rod clockwise and let the weight of the spindle twist the yarn. Draw the wool out as the spindle spins.

Yarn Sheep

Use homespun or manufactured yarn to create woolly sheep.

Vocabulary

woolly

wrap

Materials

- yarn of any color
- cardboard
- black construction paper scraps
- sheep pattern on page 155
- scissors
- black tempera paint
- glue

Project Notes

- Use yarn that children have spun to make this lesson even more rewarding.

Let's Talk About It

Where does wool come from?

What other natural fibers can be woven?

What fibers are manmade?

Steps to Follow

step 2

steps 3 & 4

1 Trace the sheep pattern onto the cardboard. Cut it out.

2 Paint both sides of the sheep with the black paint. Let it dry thoroughly.

3 Wrap the yarn around the body of the sheep, starting with the forehead and working back. Reverse directions after the shoulder. Tie a knot when the wrapping is complete.

4 Cut ears from black construction paper. Glue the ears to the sheep.

Sheep and Ear Patterns

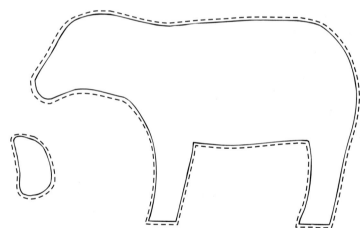

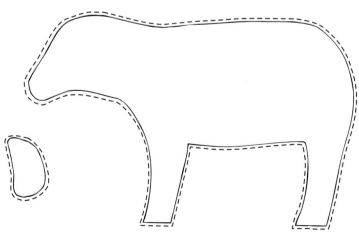

ArtWorks for Kids • EMC 761

Classroom Art Gallery

Creating pieces of art is a rewarding experience on many levels. One of those levels comes in sharing what you have created with others. Setting up a classroom (or schoolwide) "Art Gallery" provides a way for this to happen.

The size and setup of your gallery will depend on the space, equipment, and time you have. Choose among the following suggestions to create a gallery that works for you and your children.

Walls

An empty bulletin board can be transformed into a display area for both flat and three-dimensional pieces. Movable chalkboard/bulletin boards and room dividers can expand your display space.

Cover the board space with paper, cloth, burlap, wallpaper, etc., to create an interesting background. Be sure the color and texture you choose complements the pieces of artwork being displayed. Something in the wrong color can be distracting.

Frame flat pieces and pin them to the wall area in pleasing arrangements. Three-dimensional pieces such as masks can be hung on walls also. Label each piece with its title, the medium used, the artist's name, and the date created.

Ledges & Countertops

Window ledges, counter- and tabletops, and bookcases make excellent shelves on which to display three-dimensional pieces. Drape paper or cloth on the surface to add interest. Place pieces on the shelves along with labels to identify them.

Floor Areas

If you do large pieces such as papier-mâché animals, etc., set aside some floor space to use for a display. Mark the area with a rug or outline it with masking tape. Set blocks, stools, or small tables in the area to serve as stands for the pieces. Drape these with cloth. Place the pieces in the area and make a large label to identify each.

However small or expansive your gallery, invite parents and other people from the community to come and enjoy the children's work.

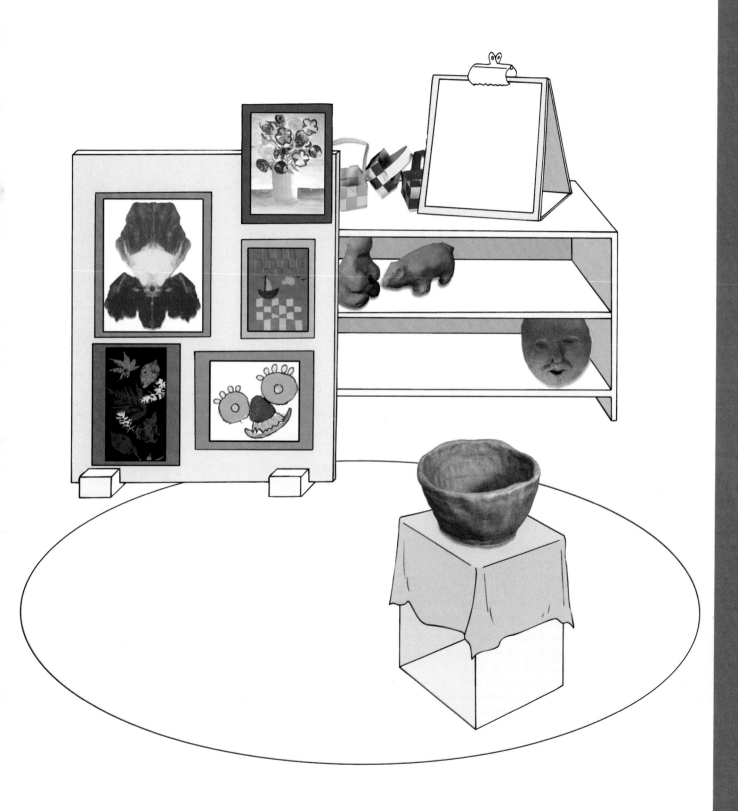

Glossary

Abstract: a design that does not project any recognizable person or thing

Action Painting: a method of painting involving movement

Arrangement: items placed in a specific order or design

Asymmetrical: not symmetrical; not capable of division into identical halves

Background: the part of a picture behind the main object or objects

Bookbinding: the cover that holds together pages of a book

Braid: to interweave three or more strands to create a plait or woven unit such as rope

Camouflage: the art of concealment; to disguise things in their surroundings

Candlewick: the string part of a candle that is lit

Carders: a set of wire-toothed brushes used to comb out fibers prior to spinning

Carving: the act of cutting wood, stone, or other material to form a figure or design

Clay: a mud-like substance with good elasticity

Collage: an artistic composition of materials and objects glued over a surface

Color: the pigment of an object

Color Scheme: a combination of colors according to a general plan

Complementary Colors: colors directly opposite each other on the color wheel (red and green, violet and yellow, blue and orange)

Cool Colors: colors that give a calming feeling (blues, greens, purples)

Craft: skill or ability in artwork done with the hands; to make by hand

Cubism: an art style characterized by geometric shapes

Deckle: the part of equipment used in making paper that has the screen to catch the fibers

Design: to prepare a plan for artwork; the overall effect of a piece of artwork

Earth Tones: colors that are readily found in nature such as browns, blues, and greens

Fantasy: an image not of the real world

Fetish: an object that is believed to have magical powers that may be carved from stone or wood

Fiber: plant, animal, or manmade tissue or material

Firing: the process of "baking" clay objects at a very high heat in a special oven called a kiln

Fixative: a spray solution applied to chalk, pastels, etc., to prevent smearing

Folk Art: traditional art of a common people

Foreground: the part of a picture nearest the spectator

Form: the design, structure, or pattern of a work of art

Free Form: a shape or artwork created without mechanical aids or guidelines

Gallery: a place that exhibits works of art

Geometric: use of simple shapes formed from straight or curved lines

Geometric Design: a plan for a painting that uses shapes

Glaze: a liquid glasslike paint used to seal and decorate clay projects

Gourd: fruit from a vine with a hard rind often of irregular shape

Graphite Transfer: a method of copying a design onto a surface with the aid of graphite; to coat the back of a drawing with graphite, then retrace

Hue: the gradation of a particular color

Impasto: a paint and paste mixture used to create texture in a painting

Impression: the effect which resembles an object or a feeling

Kiln: a type of oven that bakes clay projects at extremely high temperatures

Kimono: a long-sleeved loose robe worn by the Japanese

Landscape: a picture representing natural scenery

Limited Palette: a palette of only two or three paints

Loom: a device on which cloth is produced by interweaving thread or yarn at right angles

Luminary: a lamplike object that gives off light

Masking: the act of protecting the part of a painting not to be painted

Medium: the substance used to create a painting or print

Mixed Media: more than one medium used together on one piece of artwork

Mold: a device used in ceramics in which slip (wet clay) is poured to cast a project or clay is formed over; a form into which wax can be poured; the part of equipment used in making paper that determines the edges

Monochromatic: having only one color

Monoprint: an impression made from one source onto a surface

Mosaic: a decoration or picture made from small pieces of variously colored material

Name Chop: a carved block used in printing a signature or design

Negative Space: the space surrounding a recognizable shape

Obi: a wide sash worn with a kimono

Optical Illusion: a false appearance or impression

Origami: the Japanese art of folded paper

Paddling: a technique used in making pottery, in which a person slaps the object gently with a paddle (or similar object) to erase fingerprints and smooth lumps

Painting: the act of representing objects on a surface using paint

Paper: a material produced from pulp

Papier-Mâché: a material made from paper shreds mixed with glue that can be molded when wet and becomes hard when dry

Paraffin: a waxy, colorless mixture used to make candles

Pastels: a crayon made of pigment similar to chalk

Patterning: a design made of repeated markings

Pictograph: a picture representing an idea

Pigment: a substance used for coloring

Pinching: a method used when working with clay by pinching the clay between the fingers to form a particular shape

Positive Space: a recognizable shape

Primary Colors: the colors on the color wheel that cannot be made by mixing other colors (red, blue, yellow)

Priming: to prepare paints by adding water to soften them

Printing: the act of stamping an impression onto a surface

Pulling/ Pull-out Method a method used when working with clay by stretching the clay to form a particular shape versus adding on a separate piece of clay

Raffia: a fiber from palm leaves used for weaving baskets and mats

Realistic: an image found in the real world

Relief: the projection of forms from a flat background

Relief Print: a print made from a projection on a form

Scoring: to make lines, cuts, or notches on a surface to allow for better adherence when used with slip

Sculpture: the art of shaping a three-dimensional design by carving and/or molding

Secondary Colors: colors on the color wheel that are made from two other colors (orange, green, purple)

Shape: a definite form

Shuttle: a device used in weaving to carry the weft threads back and forth through the warp

Slip: a watery mixture of clay and water used in adhering pieces of clay together; also used in molds to cast ceramic pieces

Spin: to draw out fibers to twist into thread or yarn

Spindle:	a rod on which yarn or thread is wound
Sponging:	the act of printing or painting with a sponge
Square Knot:	a common double knot that can be achieved by tying two loose ends first right over left then left over right
Stencil:	a thin sheet with a cut pattern so that applied paint or pastel can penetrate to another surface
Still Life:	a picture consisting of inanimate objects
Symmetry/ Symmetrical:	arrangement or balancing of objects; when two sides are exactly the same
Technique:	working method of performing a particular task
Texture:	the structure, feel, and physical appearance in artwork due to the medium used
Three-Dimensional:	having depth, height, and width
Tinsmithing:	the art of making a design with light metals such as tin
Transparent:	capable of transmitting light
Warm Colors:	colors that give the feeling of warmth (reds, oranges, yellows)
Warp:	the threads that run vertically in a weaving or on a loom
Weft:	the threads that run horizontally in a weaving or on a loom
Wet on Wet Technique:	a painting technique where the paper is first wet with water, allowing the paint to blend when applied
Wick:	a cord of fibers that draws fuel to the flame as in candles
Xieyi:	(shiyĕ yī) Chinese term for freehand brushwork

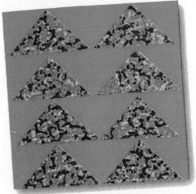